Decorative Glass

SANDBLASTING, COPPER FOIL AND LEADED STAINED GLASS

Projects & Patterns

George W. Shannon
and Pat Torlen

Sterling Publishing Co., Inc.   New York
A Sterling/Tamos Book

A Sterling/Tamos Book

Sterling Publishing Co., Inc.
387 Park Avenue South, New York, NY 10016

Tamos Books Inc.
300 Wales Avenue, Winnipeg, MB, Canada R2M 2S9

10 9 8 7 6 5 4 3 2 1

© 1999 George W. Shannon and Pat Torlen
Patterns/designs © G. W. Shannon, P. Torlen

Distributed in Canada by Sterling Publishing Co., Inc.
c/o Canadian Manda Group, One Atlantic Avenue, Suite 105
Toronto, Ontario, Canada M6K 3E7
Distributed in Great Britain and Europe by Cassell PLC,
Wellington House, 125 Strand, London WC2R 0BB, England
Distributed in Australia by Capricorn Link (Australia) Pty Ltd.
P.O. Box 6651, Baulkham Hills, Business Centre, NSW 2153,
Australia

Design Arlene Osen
Photography Jerry Grajewski & Steve Daniels,
grajewski.fotograph.inc, Wpg

Printed in China

Canadian Cataloging-in-Publication Data
Shannon, George (George Wylie), 1961–
        Decorative glass
        "A Sterling/Tamos book."
        Includes index.
        ISBN 1-895569-31-1

1. Glass craft. 2. Glass craft--Patterns.
3. Sand-blast. 4. Copper foil. I. Torlen, Pat, 1960–
II. Title.

TT298.S5385 1999   748.2'028   C98-920205-4

Library of Congress Cataloging-in Publication Data
Shannon, George, 1961–
        Decorative glass : sandblasting, copper foil and leaded
    stained glass : projects & patterns / George W. Shannon
    and Pat Torlen.
            p.   cm.
        Includes index.
        ISBN 1-895569-31-1
        1. Glass painting and staining--Patterns. 2. Glass
    etching--Patterns. 3. Sand-blast. 4. Copper foil. I. Torlen,
    Pat, 1961–. II. Title.
TT298.S38   1999   98-50984
748.6--dc21   CIP

ISBN: 1-895569-31-1

Dedication   for our students

Acknowledgments
    Special thanks to Len Dushnicky, Sue Green,
Wendy Meyer, Betty Shannon, Lynn Sinclair, and
Brianna Stark for assistance in making the
projects; Nadine Semchyshyn and Robert
Palaschuk, Marie and Robert Nagy, J. J. and Dr. T.
Kroczak, and Lynda and Jim Lawrence for
allowing us to photograph and showcase their
commissioned works; the staff of the English
Gardens, Assiniboine Park, Winnipeg, Canada for
assistance with photography locations; the
management and staff of Inkster Park Millwork
Ltd., Winnipeg, Canada for supplying the oak
frames and door units for projects in this book;
PhotoBrasive Systems, Duluth, Minnesota; and
GST Publications, Rockwood, Ontario.

Commissioned works on pages 4, 5, 8, 21, and 50 were designed and created by George W. Shannon and Pat Torlen, and attempt to show the elegance and diversity achievable using sandblasting, and copper foil and leaded stained glass construction techniques described in this book. Specific details can be obtained by contacting the Authors or the Publisher.

NOTE   If you prefer to work in metric measurements, to convert inches to millimeters multiply by 25.4.

NOTE The projects in this book are not recommended for children under the age of 12. Children ages 12 to 16 should have adult supervision when working on projects in this book.

The advice and directions given in this book have been carefully checked, prior to printing, by the Authors as well as the Publisher. Nevertheless, no guarantee can be given as to project outcome due to the possible differences in materials. Authors and Publisher will not be responsible for the results.

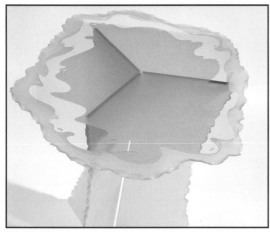

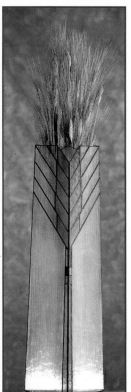

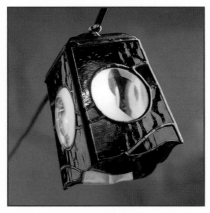

Contents

3

Introduction

Glass is one of the most versatile and useful substances known to us. It is the earliest synthetic material and has been around for nearly 4000 years, serving as articles of adornment and functioning utilities for everyday life. In ancient Egypt, where it originally flourished, glass was a luxury item used mainly for decoration.

All this changed with the discovery of glassblowing in the Eastern Roman Empire about 2000 years ago. Glassblowers used a blowpipe and other tools to form and shape molten glass into a variety of useful objects much faster than any other glass manufacturing technique.

In Europe, glassmaking skills remained below the standard of the Romans for over a thousand years. But by 1291 the Venetians had developed these skills and established a center for glassmaking on the island of Murano. Skilled craftsmen and their glassmaking secrets were closely guarded by Venetian law; nevertheless, glass industries were set up in other countries by Venetians, who influenced glassmaking styles and techniques for centuries.

Stained glass art and its fabrication were originally undertaken by skilled artisans who created small panes of translucent colored glass. This led to the introduction of stained glass windows first used in the Eastern Roman Empire in the early 12th century and began appearing in Gothic churches in Europe in the 12th to 14th centuries. These windows became intricate and awe-inspiring creations that graced the cathedrals of Europe. Over the centuries public architectural settings and the estates of the wealthy also had stained glass installations.

Periods of intense activity as well as intervals of waning interest have characterized the history of stained glass, but it has continued to evolve and flourish. This century has seen new life instilled in the art form as artists and hobbyists have embraced glass as a medium. New techniques, tools, and materials have been developed, making stained glass more accessible and affordable while allowing the medium to be pushed into new and challenging directions.

Frenchmen Emile Gallé and Eugene Rousseau were influential artists in Europe, while John LaFarge and Louis Comfort Tiffany pioneered the manufacture and use of opalescent glass in stained glass windows in the United States. A stained glass project can be crafted by utilizing the centuries-old tradition of lead came construction or by implementing the copper foil techniques first attributed to Tiffany and the glass artisans working in his studio. The fabrication method is determined by the type of design and the function of the finished piece. Lead came construction is best used for window and door panels, and larger architectural installations that have been designed with

4

The contemporary entranceway above is constructed using traditional lead came assembly techniques.

Sandblasting the glass surface creates the crisp detail evident in the dining table and buffet below.

strong graphic lines and larger pieces of glass. The glass pieces are set in lead channels that allow for some movement and flexibility in the panels should the site of the installation shift slightly or the glass pieces expand or contract due to climactic or lighting conditions. The copper foil technique requires that each piece of glass be surrounded by copper foil which is then soldered to form the infrastructure that binds the many pieces together as one unit. This results in a more rigid structure that is suitable for three-dimensional objects such as lamps, boxes, vases, etc., while maintaining the ability to create designs consisting of diverse pattern shapes and small pieces of glass. Autonomous window hangings, and interior door and window panels are frequently constructed using the copper foil technique because of its versatility, making this method increasingly popular amongst hobbyists.

Tiffany broke away from traditional methods of painting on glass to develop the copper foil technique for stained glass. He was also an innovator in techniques for blown-glass containers that had surfaces covered with an iridescent sheen. Maurice Marinot was the first artist in the art glass movement to actually design the piece and work with the glass himself. The Czechs followed after the second world war to use glass as a sculpture material to produce one-of-a-kind pieces instead of mass producing every design, and Harvey Littleton in the United States demonstrated that an individual artist could create blown glass in his own studio. As the studio glass movement grew, artists around the world began using glass as an art medium. Stained glass assumed renewed importance as an art form. It was used in windows and fixtures as part of the architectural designs of Frank Lloyd Wright and in the windows of Chartres done by Marc Chagall. As hobbyists embraced this art in the 1970s and 80s it created its own industry with retail supply shops giving stained glass classes and workshops and carrying a variety of tools and supplies for the crafter.

Another important art medium is glass etching by sandblasting. It was developed in 1870 by an American chemist and creates a smooth, evenly frosted image contrasted with clear, untouched areas of glass.

Today, artists and craftspeople can enjoy working with glass using traditional techniques and new technological advances in materials and equipment. This book offers detailed help to crafters who wish to make glass pieces that are beautiful as well as functional. There are patterns and step-by-step instructions on stained glass construction methods using lead came and copper foil as well as sandblasting techniques. The book is easy to use and offers a comprehensive guide to creating glass art for your home.

The design for the door panels is adapted from the classic hanging lotus Tiffany lamp. The panels are made using the copper foil technique attributed to Tiffany's studio.

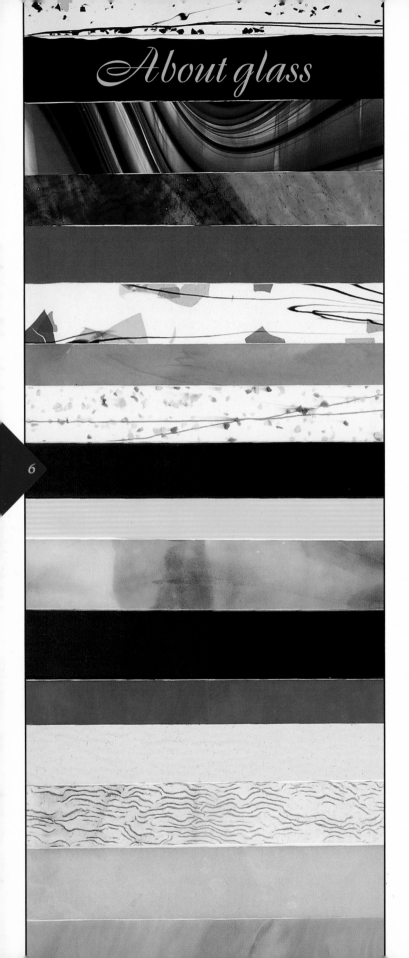

About glass

Glass is composed primarily of silica sand with smaller amounts of soda ash and lime. The basic formula has not changed much over the past 3500 years. Considered by some to be a super-cooled liquid, glass looks like a solid when in its rigid state but does not have the internal crystalline structure of solids. In its molten state, glass is malleable and flows like a liquid.

The raw materials of glass are mixed together to form batch. Molten glass is produced when the batch is heated in a furnace to temperatures ranging from 2600°F to 2900°F. The liquefied mass can be manipulated into the requisite form or shape and is then gradually cooled in a large temperature-controlled oven, called a lehr. This process, called annealing, is a period of controlled cooling to release unwanted internal stress within the glass.

Clear, flat glass used for windows is now predominately produced using the float process. A continuous flow of molten glass is drawn from the melting furnace into another one containing a bath of molten tin. Because the molten tin is perfectly smooth and level, the ribbon of glass becomes flat and uniform in thickness as it "floats" over the tin. The glass is carefully cooled until it reaches a solid state and can be guided from the still-molten tin bath to an annealing oven without damaging the glass surface. The float process does not require grinding and polishing of the glass surface. It produces glass that is uniformly even and has a brilliant fire-polished surface on both sides. Float glass is ideal for the decorative sandblasting techniques used in several of the projects in this book.

Stained glass is produced in various colors by adding metal oxides to the batch. Lead oxides are introduced to add brilliancy and clarity. Cobalt and chromium produce shades of blue, while adding manganese to cobalt blue results in purple. Red, orange, and yellow contain selenium and cadmium, and copper is added for black, green, or red glass. Gold oxides produce beautiful and expensive gold-pinks. Temperature and iron content in the batch also play a role in the shades and colors achieved.

Rich, translucent sheets of stained glass can be created using age-old glassblowing techniques. Glassblowers pick molten glass up out of the furnace on the end of a blowpipe and a cylindrical shape is blown. It is then rotated in a mold to even the surface and create the striations unique to antique glass. The ends are cut off and the cylinder is cut lengthwise, allowing it to flatten and form a sheet of glass.

Machine-rolled glass is known for its consistency in color and thickness. Molten glass is continuously fed through sets of metal rollers and onto a slow-moving conveyer-type line. As the glass passes through the roller, patterns and textures can be embossed on the surface before the ribbon of glass reaches the annealing lehr.

Hand-cast glass is produced one sheet at a time. Molten glass is ladled onto a metal table and rolled by hand to the desired thickness. Interesting sheets of glass can be produced by mixing in swirls of different colors, thin glass rods, and shards of colored glass before the sheet of glass is transferred to the lehr.

Types of glass

Sheets of stained glass are commonly referred to as art glass and are predominantly produced in Europe and the United States. Glass is available in countless and unique color and texture combinations.

Full-antique Handmade using glassblowing techniques; characterized by rich coloring, translucency, and surface striations; varies in color and uniformity and has trapped air pockets and bubbles.

Semi-antique Machine-made, translucent, of a single color, consistent thickness, with surface striations.

Architectural Smooth on one side, textured on the other; 4mm to 6mm thick; usually clear; some patterns available in bronze or amber; can be substituted for clear float glass in windows, doors, room dividers, sidelights, etc.

Cathedral Translucent; often a single color; machine-rolled or mouth-blown.

Craquel Full-antique glass that is dipped in cool water causing exterior layer of glass to "crack" forming surface alligator-like pattern.

Flashed Antique glass; has second color layer on top of base color which can be exposed by sandblasting or acid etching away parts of the top layer to create design.

Fractures and streamers "Confetti" glass has shards of colored glass and thin glass rods added to a clear or opal base sheet—(used by Tiffany to represent distant foliage in window panels and for lamps).

Glue chip Animal hide glue is applied to cathedral glass that has been sandblasted on one side, then placed in warming oven; as glue dries, it tears away flakes of glass from sheet's surface, creating a pattern.

Iridescent Cathedral or opalescent glass; surface coated with ultra-thin layer of metallic salts during manufacturing to produce shimmering finish.

Mirror Sheets of clear float glass and colored art glass (usually semi-antique) coated with reflective silver backing to create mirror.

Opalescent Has milky, luminesce appearance; combination of 2 or more tones or colors; often used in stained glass lamp shades.

Opaque Transmits little light; single color or 2 or more colors swirled together; popular choice for creating stained glass mosaics.

Ring mottled Hand-cast opalescent glass has hazy surface covering small circular patterns within the glass; used in glass mosaics, Tiffany-style lamp shades, and nature-theme window panels.

Seedy Cathedral glass with smooth surface and small air bubbles dispersed throughout.

Streaky Swirls of 2 or more colors mixed but not blended together.

Textured Ripple, hammered, granite, crystal ice, herringbone, ribbed, fibroid, moss, flemish, muffle, and cube textures made by art glass manufacturers.

Bevels Angled border approximately ½ in wide is ground and polished on the topside edges of a clear glass piece to refract light.

Jewels Gem-like pieces of pressed glass, usually faceted; available in a selection of shapes and colors.

Glass nuggets Small pieces of glass, irregular in shape and size, sometimes called globs.

Rondels Translucent circular pieces of glass made by spinning molten glass on the end of a glassblower's punty rod.

Stained Glass Construction & Sandblasting

To complete the stained glass projects in this book you will need materials and tools commonly found around the home plus some specifically designed for crafting stained glass. Most urban centers have at least one retail outlet that caters to stained glass craftspeople, and several companies offer a mail order service.

The instruction on sandblasting focuses on the skills required to prepare glass so that a design can be sandblasted onto its surface. If you don't have sandblasting equipment, the prepared glass pieces can be taken to a local stained glass shop or a window and auto glass supplier for the actual sandblasting. The techniques shown can also be used to provide more detail to many stained glass projects. You can purchase the float glass and mirror required for several of the sandblasting projects at a window and auto glass supplier, stained glass shop, or mail order service (check your telephone directory yellow pages). If a friend has worked with stained glass or done sandblasting, ask for recommendations. A wide selection of tools and materials is available.

Materials used

Resist materials Areas not to be sandblasted are covered with vinyl or rubber resist with an adhesive backing, that is adhered to the glass. Designs are cut into the resist with a stencil or utility knife. Thick automotive masking tapes, hot glue, cheesecloth, stickers and labels, can also be used.

Came Extruded 6 ft lengths of channeled lead, zinc, brass, or copper, available in many styles, used to assemble leaded glass windows or as a border on copper foil panels.

Copper foil Adhesive-backed copper foil tape is wrapped around cut pieces of glass and then soldered to provide a support structure. Foil comes in 36 yd rolls, and is available in a variety of widths with copper, silver, or black backing.

Flux Liquid, paste, gel, or cream flux is applied to copper foil and came joints to help solder fuse to these surfaces.

Solder This alloy of tin and lead, produced as $\frac{1}{8}$ in thick wire, will fuse to lead came and copper foil when flux and heat are applied (approximately 600°F to 800°F). Use **60/40** (60% tin and 40% lead) to make rounded solder joints or seams; **50/50** (equal parts tin and lead) to form a basecoat on seams of 3-dimensional objects; and **lead free** (mainly tin) for stained glass jewelry.

Reinforcement materials Steel or zinc reinforcement bars (rebar) are soldered to exterior seams or joints; re-strip (strong, flexible copper strips) add strength to foiled glass pieces.

Cement and whiting Putty-like cement seals and strengthens the leaded glass panel. Whiting (calcium carbonate) removes excess cement and flux, and polishes glass surface.

Vase cap Made of spun brass with several small vent holes to allow heat to escape; holds individual lamp shade panels together.

Spider Small brass ring has 3 or 4 spoke-like arms to give lamp shade support and a means to suspend it from a ceiling fixture or on a lamp base.

Hinges and fine-linked chain A brass tube and the rod that fits within it, creates a hinge; a length of fine-link chain helps secure the lid to a stained glass box and prevents breakage.

Tinned copper wire Copper wire (14 to 20 gauge with or without tin coating) adds strength to small projects and makes loops for hanging panels and small projects.

Patina Solution of water, copper sulfates, and mineral acids applied to solder seam to change surface to a copper or black finish. Used on copper foil projects.

Neutralizing solution Mixture of water, sodium bicarbonate, and a sudsing agent used to neutralize and wash away excess flux and patina.

Finishing wax Can be a stained glass finishing compound or quality car wax used to protect solder seams of finished stained glass projects.

$\frac{3}{4}$ in plywood, wood trim, and nails Used to assemble lead came and copper foil projects.

Equipment used

Permanent fine-tipped marker Used to outline pattern pieces on glass.

Drawing equipment small square, pencil, eraser, cork-backed ruler or straightedge, grid paper, tracing paper, carbon paper, marking pen, compass, scissors, light cardstock.

Utility knife and/or stencil knife Used to cut designs in sandblasting resist, trim copper foil, cut out paper pattern pieces, etc.

Squeegee Smooths resist flat against a glass surface to prevent air bubbles.

Pattern shears Have 3 blades to cut out pattern pieces for templates while removing the necessary space between the pattern pieces to allow for solder or lead came.

Glass cutters Can be dry-wheel or oil-fed and used to score and break individual pieces of glass to fit the project pattern. Larger wheel disposable cutters must be lubricated before each score. Self-lubricating cutters have smaller cutting wheels and have a reservoir for oil. They are more expensive but more accurate and last for many years. Popular models have either a traditional pencil-shaped barrel or a pistol grip handle.

Breaking, grozing, and combination pliers Break off scored pieces of glass; breaking pliers have flat smooth jaws to grip and break off glass; grozing pliers have narrow, flat, serrated jaws to nibble edge of glass; combination pliers have top jaw that is flat and bottom jaw that is concave—both are serrated.

Running pliers Apply equal pressure on both sides of a long straight score line forcing it to break along its length. **Metal** (preferred) have a concave jaw (placed on top side of glass) and a convex jaw (placed on underside of glass) that allows the breaking of narrow pieces of glass. **Plastic** have 3 teeth—2 on top jaw and one on lower jaw.

Carborundum stone Block of hard carbon and silicon files sharp edges off glass. Must be kept wet to keep minute glass particles from becoming airborne.

Wet/dry sandpaper Has a silicon carbide coating that can be used to take the sharpness off cut glass edges. Must be wet when used on glass.

Glass grinder Has a diamond coated bit to grind the edge on a glass piece, and a reservoir containing water to trap the dust produced when grinding.

Lead came cutters and lead knives Used for a clean, even cut that does not crush the channels of the came. Lead came cutters (knippers or lead dykes) look like pliers but have a set of sharp, pointed jaws that are ground flat on one side. A lead knife has a sharp, curved blade and cuts using a rocking back-and-forth motion.

Lead vise Used to clamp one end of the came while the lead is being pulled from the other end with a pair of pliers to straighten it.

Lathekin or fid Used to open up and widen the channels of any type of came.

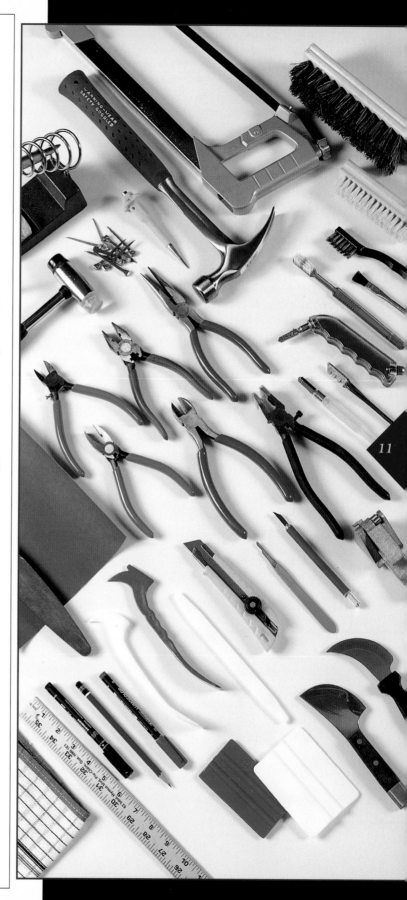

11

Horseshoe or glaziers nails   Flat-sided nails used to hold lead came and pieces of stained glass in position.

Glazing hammer   Head has 2 different ends—softer rubber to tap glass pieces into place and plastic to drive horseshoe nails into work surface or project board.

Soldering iron, sponge, and stand   Iron is used to melt solder to join the pieces of a copper foiled project together and bond together the lead came pieces at each juncture of a leaded panel. The iron has a chisel-shaped tip; should be between 80 and 150 watts (100 watts best for hobbyists), and must be able to maintain a constant and even temperature (600°F to 900°F). Can have a built-in temperature control or can be regulated by a rheostat. Needs a stand and sponge made of natural fibers to clean the tip during soldering process.

Sidecutters   Can cut wire, chain, and zinc or brass came (not suitable for lead came).

Hacksaw   Cuts thicker brass or zinc cames.

Needlenose pliers   Used to hold small loops, chains, etc. in position while soldering.

Brushes   Small brushes for applying flux; wire brushes for scraping oxidation from surface of lead came; soft bristled scrub brushes for cementing and cleaning leaded panels; old toothbrushes for applying patina and cleaning projects.

Polishing cloths   Clean, dry (cotton preferred); for buffing.

Woodworking tools   used to install completed panels into cabinets, door or window frames, room dividers, etc.

12

Work area

Choose a comfortable working space with enough room to spread out the project. A working area requires

• Large, sturdy table or workbench at comfortable working height around waist high with a smooth, level work surface (preferably plywood).
• Overhead lighting (natural light if possible).
• Electrical outlet with grounded circuit for soldering iron and glass grinder.
• Easy-to-clean hard-surfaced floor.
• Rack or wooden bin with dividers to store sheets of glass in an upright position (store smaller pieces in a cardboard box).
• Good ventilation (window, fan) when soldering, working with patinas, cements, and whiting.
• Newspaper to cover work surface for easy cleaning.
• Bench brush and dust pan to clear work surface.
• Water to rinse off sandblasting grit when using glass grinder or carborundum stone, and for cleaning projects.
• Storage box for lengths of lead came. If box does not close, cover with newspaper to reduce oxidation. Ask your local stained glass shop for an empty came box.
• Storage box (sealable) for lead came scraps. Keep away from children. When the box is full take it to a depot that recycles lead. Do not throw into regular garbage.
• Light table for tracing patterns onto hard-to-see-through glass.

Building a light table   Make a plywood box with a fluorescent fixture placed inside and ¼ in (6mm) clear float glass for the top. The underside of the glass must be sandblasted to diffuse light from the bulbs. (Most shops selling float glass will do this.) Paint inside of plywood box for better light reflection.

NOTE If you don't have a light table, trace patterns onto smaller pieces of glass by taping the pattern onto an outside-facing window. Place the glass on top of the pattern, and trace the pattern onto the glass. This method is not recommended for large pieces of glass.

NOTE Keep glass chips and other debris in a separate, sturdy box.

Safety practices & equipment

While sandblasting or working with stained glass use these 4 items when appropriate: safety glasses or goggles, work apron, rubber or latex gloves, respirator or dust mask.

Follow these common sense rules for a safe and healthy work environment.

• Wear safety glasses or goggles when cutting glass, soldering, or using chemicals to prevent the risk of injury to eyes.

• Do not eat, drink, or smoke while working with stained glass. Keep hands away from mouth and face while working. Wash hands, arms, and face thoroughly with soap and water at the end of a work session.

• Wear rubber or latex gloves when leading a panel, handling patinas, and cementing compounds.

• Cover all cuts and scrapes with an adhesive plaster when working with lead, solder, or chemicals. Lead is not usually absorbed through the skin but can enter through open sores and cuts. Fluxes and patinas can irritate broken skin.

• Wear a full length work apron to protect clothes and prevent the spread of glass fragments, lead particles, and sandblasting dust and grit from entering your living space. Wash work clothes and aprons separately from other clothing.

• Wear closed shoes to protect your feet from glass fragments and molten solder.

• Wear a dust mask or respirator when cementing and using whiting on leaded windows, restoring old stained glass windows, sandblasting, or extensive soldering on stained glass projects.

• Clear the work surface often with a bench brush and clean the floor with a damp mop or wet sponge. Avoid sweeping and vacuuming (particles will become airborne).

• Carry glass in a vertical position with one hand supporting the sheet from below and the other hand steadying the sheet from the side. Wear protective gloves when moving larger sheets.

NOTE Young children should not work with stained glass unless supervised by an experienced adult. Pregnant women are advised to check with their physician.

Soldering safety Lead fumes are produced in such minute quantities at the temperatures required for stained glass soldering, that there is little danger of lead contamination through inhalation. However, some mist is produced as the flux is burned off during soldering. Apply only the amount of flux needed. Excessive flux will give off unnecessary fumes and may cause the solder to spatter and spit, creating pits in the solder seam and possibly burning your hands. The mist is generally considered harmless; nevertheless, you should work in a well ventilated area with a small fan positioned so that the mist is pulled away from you. Or you can wear a respirator with filters designed to screen out mists and vapors. Avoid fluxes containing zinc chloride and hydrochloric acids. Always rest hot soldering irons in a metal stand, never on a work surface. Do not leave a plugged-in iron unattended.

Lead safety Never have food, drink, or cigarettes in a work area. Keep hands away from mouth and face when soldering or leading stained glass panels. Always wash hands, arms, and face thoroughly with soap and water. Wear rubber or latex gloves when leading and discard when the project is finished. Always cover cuts and scrapes with an adhesive bandage. Do not leave lead scraps lying about. Store scraps in a separate container used only for lead. Scrub work surfaces with soap and water and wipe with paper towels that can be discarded immediately. Keep lead out of the reach of small children and inform older ones of the safety rules.

Sandblasting safety The main safety concern when sandblasting is the dust (airborne particles and silica dust) that is produced. Silicosis is an incurable respiratory disease caused by the inhalation of silica dust over an extended period of time and though there is little risk to the hobbyist, care should be taken to reduce the amount of exposure.

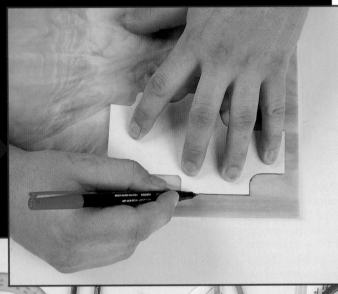

Place translucent glass on pattern copy and trace piece to be cut.

Cut out individual pattern pieces and trace onto opaque glass.

Basic techniques

Making copies of the patterns Make 2 or 3 copies of the pattern for each stained glass or sandblasting project. Most patterns can be altered if a specific size or shape is desired. Be sure all copies are accurate before starting the project. Remember to allow space between each piece of stained glass for its support structure. The thickness of the design lines should be $\frac{1}{16}$ in for leaded panels and $\frac{1}{32}$ in for copper foil projects. Use a marking pen with the appropriate size nib to draw the pattern lines. Some stained glass projects use pre-cut bevels and jewels. Verify that they fit the pattern before cutting the other glass pieces required.

For sizing reference, patterns in this book that are not full size are placed on grid work, 1 square = 1 inch.

Photocopying Be sure to verify each copy with the original pattern, especially for 3-dimensional projects. Many photocopiers can also enlarge or reduce patterns.

Tracing Lay tracing vellum over the pattern and trace the lines of the design. For multiple copies lay a sheet of paper on the work surface and place a carbon face down overtop (repeat this for each copy required). Place the project pattern on top and fasten in place, using push pins or tape. Trace the outline of the pattern, pressing firmly so that the image is transferred through to each layer of paper.

Grid method Use a grid to enlarge, reduce, or change the dimensions of a design. On paper large enough to accommodate the desired size, draw a new grid work with the size of the squares adjusted to fit the new grid. Copy the design from the original grid onto the modified one, square by square.

Blueprinting The pattern is traced onto drawing vellum and taken to a blueprinting firm to make exact copies. If a pattern requiring bevels or jewels of a specific size and/or shape is reduced or enlarged, verify that these pieces fit the pattern before starting the project. Alter the pattern if necessary.

Overhead and opaque projectors These can be used to enlarge pattern designs, but they often distort the image. We recommend using this method as a guideline only. When enlarging patterns containing pieces that must be a certain size, the pattern will have to be altered accordingly.

Transferring the pattern onto glass Draw the outline of the piece to be cut directly onto the glass with a permanent waterproof fine-tipped marker. Position to avoid excessive waste and accommodate the grain or texture of the other glass pieces around it. Leave approximately $\frac{1}{4}$ in around the piece so the breaking pliers will have some material to grasp when breaking the score line.

For translucent and light-colored opalescent glasses transfer the pattern by placing the sheet of glass directly on the pattern copy and tracing the design lines with the marker. A light box will help illuminate the pattern from below, but it is not essential.

For opaque glass the pattern can be transferred onto the glass using one of these 3 methods:

1 Cut out the required pattern piece from an extra copy of the pattern making sure the design line is removed. If you use stained glass pattern shears be sure to use the appropriate pair for the type of project (copper foil or leaded glass). Place the pattern piece on the glass and trace around the outside edges with the marker.

2 Make a template (cardstock or lightweight cardboard) of the pieces to be cut (using the tracing method described on p14) and trace around the template onto the glass. This method is preferable when making several projects using the same pattern.

3 Place a carbon sheet face down on the glass with the pattern on top. By pressing firmly on the lines with a pen or pencil, the pattern will be transferred onto the glass. Go over the carbon lines with the marker.

> **NOTE** When cutting out a piece from the pattern copy or making a cardboard template, be sure to cut on the **inside** of the pattern lines.

Cutting glass—basics

Cutting glass is the result of scoring and breaking. The required shape is traced onto the glass with a permanent marker, and scored by running the wheel of a glass cutter along the traced line. By applying even pressure on either side of the score line, the piece is broken away from the main sheet of glass.

Draw cutting patterns A, B, C, and D (p16) on 3mm float glass (windowpane glass) and practice the techniques of scoring and breaking before starting your first project. Follow these guidelines.

1 Wear safety glasses and work apron. Stand in upright position in front of worktable.

2 Work on a clean, level, non-skid work surface covered with newspaper.

3 Place the glass smooth side up, showing traced pattern. Make sure the surface of the glass is clean and free of debris.

4 Lubricate the wheel of the glass cutter before each score if it is not self-oiling. Use an oil designed specifically for glass cutters or a lightweight machine oil (sewing machine oil).

5 Hold the cutter in your writing hand, perpendicular to the glass, not tilted to the left or right. Steady the glass sheet with your opposite hand on the other side of the line you wish to score.

6 Run cutter away from your body along inside of pattern lines, applying steady pressure from your shoulder. Start score line at one edge of glass and follow through to another edge. Do not stop or lift cutter from glass surface before score is completed. Try not to run cutter off the edge of glass sheet. You will be able to hear cutter score glass and the score line

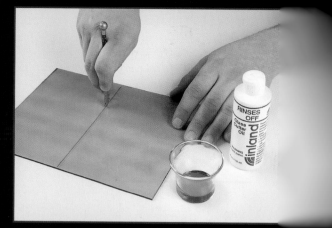

Disposable cutter held in traditional manner. Cutter rests between index and middle fingers with ball thumb placed to push cutter along. Disposable cutters wear quickly and cutting wheel must be lubricated before each score.

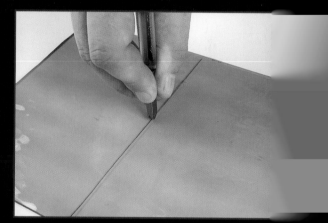

Oil-fed pencil style cutter is held like a pencil.

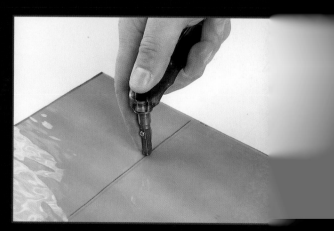

Pistol grip cutter held in palm of hand with thumb resting on barrel and index finger guiding cutter head.

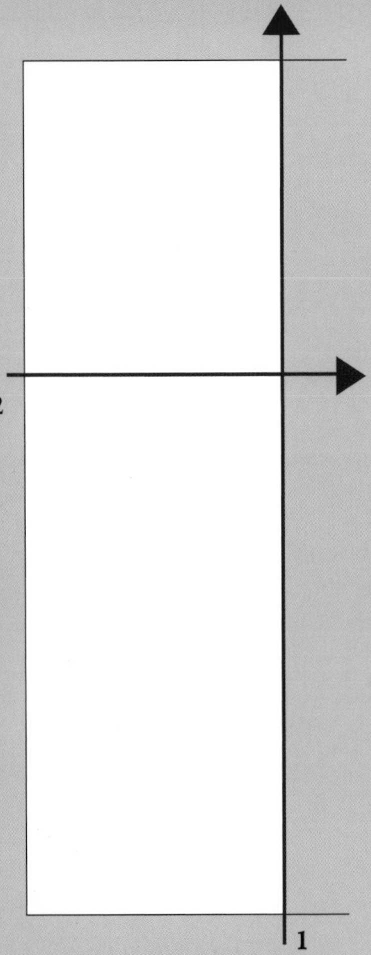

16

Pattern A—square/rectangles

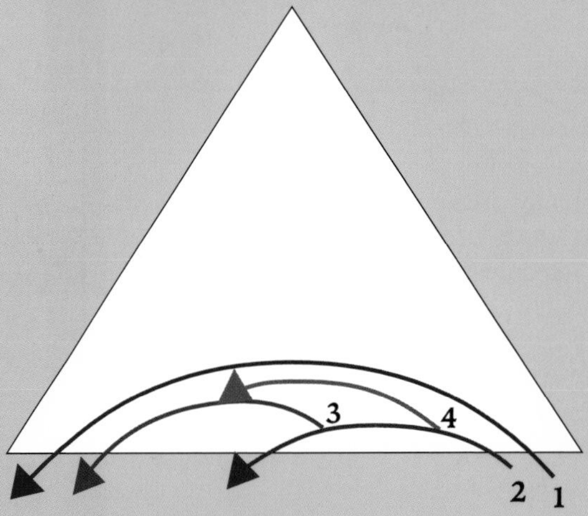

2

1

Pattern B—inside curves

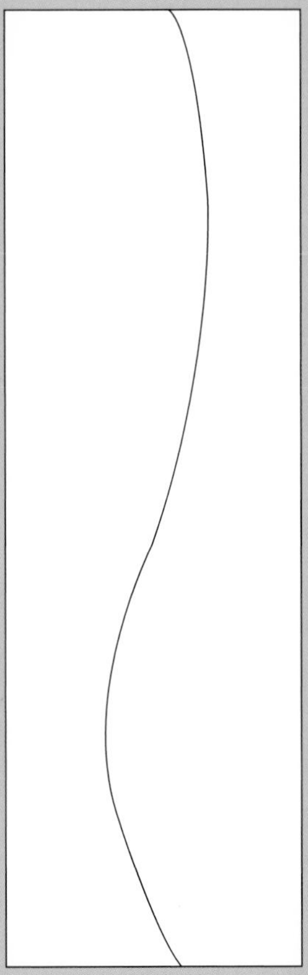

3   4

2   1

Pattern D—
S-shaped curve

5   6

Pattern C—oval

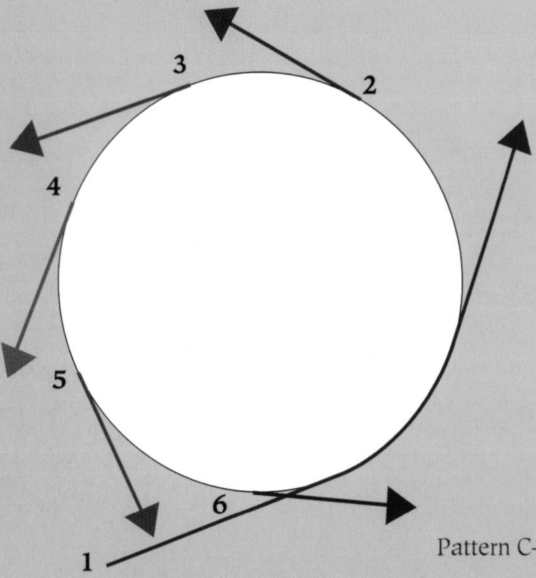

4   3

2   1

Pattern C—circle

3   2

4

5

6

1

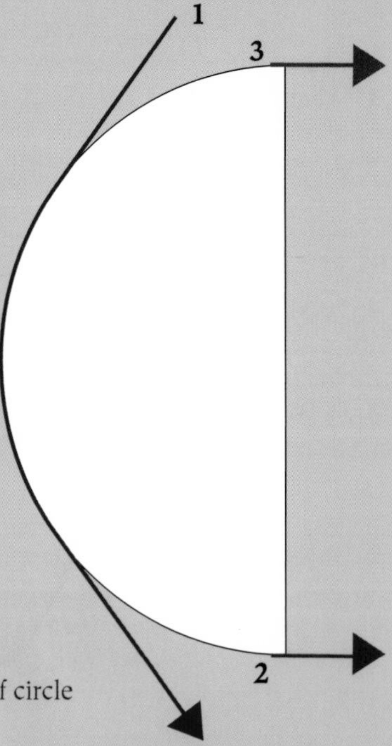

Pattern C—half circle

1   3

2

will be visible to the eye. If small white slivers are present along score line, too much pressure has been applied.

7 Never go over a score line a second time. It will damage cutter wheel and break may not be successful.

8 Complete the break by grasping the glass with a hand on each side of score line, thumbs parallel to score, knuckles touching. Roll wrists up and outward, breaking along score line.

9 Maintain the glass cutter. Keep the cutter wheel oiled and covered when not in use. Periodically, check that the reservoir of your self-oiling cutter has a sufficient amount of oil in it. Wipe away any small glass fragments that may have collected on the cutter wheel.

To break glass, grasp glass on each side of scored line and roll wrists up and outward.

Breaking glass on a score line (additional methods)

Using running pliers   for breaking straight lines, slight curves, and starting a break at either end of a score line. Metal pliers are preferred. Place concave jaw on topside of glass and convex jaw below. For plastic pliers, position jaw with the 2 outside "teeth" or ridges on topside of glass.

1 Position the running pliers so that the score line is centered and the glass is partially inside the jaws, approximately ½ in to ¾ in.

2 Gently squeeze the handles and the score will "run" (travel), causing the glass to break off into 2 pieces. If the run does not go the full length of the score line, repeat the procedure at the other end of the score line. The 2 "runs" should meet, causing the score line to break completely.

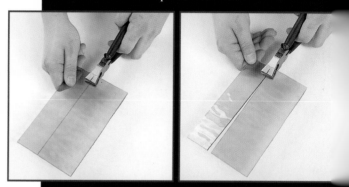

Use running pliers for breaking straight lines or slight curves.

Using breaking pliers or combination pliers   Breaking pliers have identical flat jaws that can be placed on either side of glass. Combination pliers have a flat top jaw and a curved bottom jaw—both are serrated.

1 Position pliers perpendicular to score line and as close as possible without touching it. Start at either end of score line (not the middle).

2 Use an out-and-downward pulling motion on the pliers to break the glass.

3 When using 2 sets of pliers to break apart smaller pieces of glass, place the pliers on the glass on either side of the score line and opposite to each other. Hold one set of pliers steady and use an out-and-downward pulling motion with the other set to separate the glass piece.

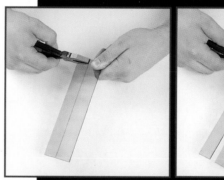

Position jaws of breaking pliers or combination pliers perpendicular to score line.

Tapping   may be required for a long or curving score line.

1 Hold the glass close to the surface of the worktable. Using the ball at the end of the cutter, gently strike the glass from the underside, directly underneath the score line. Once the score begins to "run," continue tapping ahead of the run until it reaches the other end of the score line.

2 With your hands or a pair of pliers, separate the scored piece from the main sheet of glass.

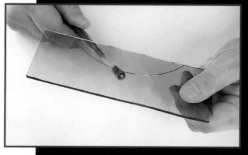

Tap ahead of the "run" until score line is broken o[...]

> **NOTE**   Use tapping method with care, to break out stubborn pieces.

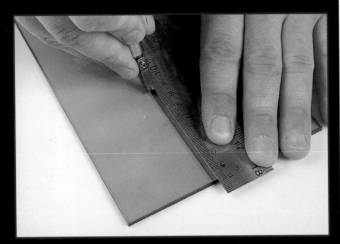

Use straightedge to guide cutter when scoring straight lines.

Align score line with edge of worktable. Snap off end of glass with swift, downward motion.

Scoring a straight line

1 Mark the line to be cut and position a cork-backed metal ruler or straightedge parallel and approximately ⅛ in from the line (the exact distance is determined by the space between the cutter wheel and the outside edge of the cutter head).

2 Align head of glass cutter with straightedge on the line.

3 Holding straightedge firmly on glass surface, make score line by pulling cutter toward the body or pushing it away. Maintain even pressure.

4 Break the score line, using the method you prefer (p17).

Cutting large sheets of glass

1 Check the pattern to determine how large a piece of glass you will need. Score the sheet, using a straightedge as a guide for the glass cutter.

2 Align the score line with the edge of the worktable.

3 Grasp glass firmly with both hands, raise end of sheet, about 1 in from table surface. The opposite end of sheet must still be in contact with table.

4 With a swift, downward motion, snap off the end of the piece.

Cutting squares and rectangles

1 Trace pattern A (p16) onto glass, aligning one side of pattern with edge of glass.

2 Score along other side of pattern piece and break the score line, (p17).

3 Score and break any remaining cut required on pattern piece.

> **NOTE** Because it is almost impossible to cut glass at a 90° angle, use a series of straight scores and breaks for cutting square and rectangular pieces.

Cutting squares and rectangles requires several straight score lines and breaks.

Cutting inside curves

1 Trace pattern piece B (p16) onto glass, aligning outer edges of curve with edge of the glass.

2 Score the inside curve of the pattern piece.

3 Make several smaller concave score lines (scallops) between initial score line and outside edge of glass.

4 Using breaker or combination pliers, remove scallops, one at a time, beginning with the one closest to the edge of the glass. Use a pulling action with the pliers rather than a downward motion. Position jaws of pliers at either end of score line, not in the middle.

5 Continue to break away the scallops until you reach the initial score line. Remove it and proceed to score and break away the pattern piece from the larger glass sheet.

Cutting circles, ovals, and outside curves

1 Trace circle pattern C (p16) onto the glass, leaving ½ in from the outside edge of the glass.

2 Make an initial score line that will separate the pattern piece from the sheet of glass. The score line will go from the outside edge of the glass and upon reaching the circle will follow the perimeter of it for a short distance and then head off on a tangent to an opposite edge of the glass (see line 1). Break away this piece.

3 Score the second line to follow around the circle for a short distance (approximately ⅙ th of the perimeter) and then leave on a tangent to the outside edge (see line 2).

4 Repeat step 3, scoring and breaking the glass in a pinwheel fashion, until the circle shape has been formed (see lines 3, 4, 5, and 6).

5 Cut outside curves and ovals by adapting this method used for cutting circular pieces.

Scoring and breaking S-shaped curves

1 Trace pattern D (p16) onto the glass, placing one side against the edge of the glass.

2 Score the most difficult cut first (S-shape).

3 Align the running pliers with the score line. Squeeze only hard enough to start the run. Repeat the procedure at the opposite end of the score line. If both runs meet, use your hands to separate the resulting 2 pieces. If the runs do not meet, gently tap along the score line (on the underside of the glass).

4 Score and break out remaining cuts.

NOTE Inside curves are the most difficult cuts to score and break. Attempt these first before breaking the piece away from the main sheet of glass.

Cutting a piece with inside curves requires a series of cuts.

Cut piece away from main sheet of glass before scoring and breaking the glass in a pinwheel fashion.

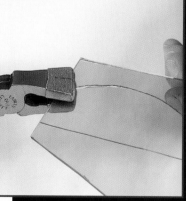

Start "run" at one end of score line. Then start "run" at opposite end of score line.

Separate into two pieces and score and break out remaining cuts.

Jagged edges of glass can be smoothed by grozing.

Keep glass piece, wet/dry sandpaper, and carborundum stone wet while smoothing edges.

Glass grinders can be used to shape difficult-to-cut glass pieces.

Smoothing jagged edges of glass

Use a glass grinder, pliers, a carborundum stone, or wet/dry sandpaper to smooth jagged edges or shape glass pieces.

Grozing Grasp the piece of glass firmly in one hand, place the combination pliers perpendicular to the edge of the glass, and drag the serrated jaws along the jagged edge in an up-and-down motion. Repeat until the edge is relatively smooth.

Using a carborundum stone or wet/dry sandpaper

1 Wet the carborundum stone or wet/dry sandpaper and the piece of glass with water.

2 Rub moist stone or sandpaper in a file-like motion along edge of moist glass until smooth.

3 Rinse glass and stone or paper under running water to wash away glass residue.

Using a glass grinder

1 Attach a face shield to grinder and position a back splash along back and sides of grinder to contain any airborne chips and water overspray.

2 Keep water in the reservoir and have a moistened sponge positioned adjacent to the diamond-coated bit at all times.

3 Cut each glass piece on the inside of the pattern line to fit the pattern with a minimum of grinding and allow space for lead came or copper foil between each piece. If the glass pieces fit within and do not overlap the pattern lines, make one quick swipe against the grinding bit on each edge of the glass to dull any sharpness. Only light pressure is required when pushing the glass against the bit.

4 If traces of the marked line are still visible on the piece, grind the edge to ensure an accurate fit within the pattern lines.

5 Check each piece against the pattern. If any part of the piece overlaps and there is not adequate spacing between the pattern pieces, mark the area with a permanent marker and grind away the excess until the piece fits.

6 Repeat steps 3 through 5 for each piece. Pieces that leave a large gap between the line and the adjacent piece should be recut.

7 Rinse each piece under clear running water and dry with a soft cloth. Do not allow pattern copy to get wet.

8 Wipe surface of grinder often with a wet sponge to prevent glass chips from scratching the underside of pieces being ground. Do not run bare hands across the grinder's grid surface.

9 Clean grinder thoroughly and rinse the water reservoir at the end of each work session.

NOTE A glass grinder is recommended for stained glass but is not necessary for the sandblasting projects in this book. Precise glass cutting of copper foil projects will lessen the need for grinding.

Helpful hint Keep smaller patterns dry during the grinding stage by placing them inside vinyl sheet protectors or covering them with an adhesive-backed clear vinyl.

Sandblasting

Etching glass

Elegant, frosted images can be inscribed onto the surface of most glass objects by either acid etching or sandblasting. Hydrofluoric acid eats away at exposed areas to leave a satin matte finish; however, the acid is a hazardous chemical with toxic fumes that must be used in a controlled environment (safer diluted etching cream formulas for use by hobbyists often produce a blotchy, uneven finish). The other choice, sandblasting, produces the most consistent results. It is the propulsion of an abrasive material, under high air pressure and velocity, at an object that has been partially covered with a protective material called resist to produce a frosted design. Sandblasting deeper into the glass and using various resist materials create different effects.

Originally used for industrial purposes, sandblasting is now embraced by craftspeople and artisans working in glass. Any design style or image can be used or adapted to suit the project at hand. The skills outlined in this book are an introduction to surface sandblasting (single-stage blasting) that forms the basis for more advanced methods—multiple-stage blasting and sandcarving. Detailed instruction includes preparing the glass, applying and hand cutting resist materials, and methods used to sandblast the desired image. Once prepared (the major part of the procedure), the glass pieces can be taken to a local stained glass shop or a window and auto glass center for the actual sandblasting if you don't own your own sandblasting equipment. Alternatively, many stained glass studios offer classes and will rent time on their equipment to experienced craftspeople who wish to do the sandblasting themselves.

Photo courtesy of PhotoBrasive Systems, Duluth, MN

Incubator-style sandblasting cabinet with exhaust system.

How-to techniques

Equipment & abrasives

If you are considering investing in your own sandblasting system, you will need an electric air compressor, a blasting cabinet or booth, a receptacle for the abrasive, heavy-duty hoses for air and the abrasive, and a blast gun or nozzle assembly to direct the spray of abrasive. Two different systems can be used for sandblasting—the siphon system and pressure-pot system. We recommend the pressure-pot system. Sandblasting takes less time, air and abrasive are easily controlled and adjusted, and a smaller air compressor is sufficient to operate it.

Siphon system   Requires a spray gun fitted with 2 hoses, connecting it to the air compressor and the hopper containing the abrasive. Compressed air, traveling at high velocity, is transported through a hose that is connected to the base of the gun. As air is forced through the gun towards the nozzle, it passes over the opening of the second hose. A vacuum is created and the abrasive is drawn up through the hose connected to the bottom of the hopper. The mixture of compressed air and abrasive is then propelled through the nozzle and blasted towards the glass. Air pressure of 80 to 110 PSI (pounds per square inch) is needed and requires a powerful air compressor, usually 5 to 10 HP (horsepower).

Pressure-pot system   Compressed air is fed directly into a pressure-tested, steel container (pot) filled with abrasive. Air and abrasive is then forced out of the pressurized pot and through another hose to the nozzle assembly. Air flow and abrasive can be easily adjusted. Air pressure (20 to 40 PSI) is required so most systems can be operated using a 2 to 5 HP air compressor.

Blasting cabinet   A well-designed, enclosed incubator-style sandblasting cabinet has a vacuum exhaust and dust collection system. It must be well lit, have a sizeable observation window, a door that seals tightly, and be large enough to provide easy access when transferring glass in and out of the cabinet. The front wall of the cabinet has 2 armholes fitted with thick rubber gloves that extend into the cabinet. A hopper or collection bin at the bottom of the cabinet allows for recycling and removal of the abrasive. Larger projects will require a walk-in booth.

Abrasives   Aluminum oxide and silicon carbide are available in a variety of grits (80 to 120 are commonly used). **Aluminum oxide** is economical, can be recycled many times, and is used throughout the glass industry. However, it does generate some static electricity causing it to cling to the glass. **Silicon carbide** is more expensive, can be used many times, creates little static, and does not dull as it breaks down. During sandblasting, a small beam of light is produced when the abrasive particles strike the glass and each other, making it easier to see exactly where the stream of abrasive is hitting the glass.

> NOTE **Sand** is still used by some hobbyists, but is not recommended because it breaks down into very fine particles, creating silica dust, which over time may cause silicosis, an incurable lung disease. Furthermore, blasting time is greatly increased because sand particles dull quickly and can only be used once or twice.

Safety guidelines

• Wear safety glasses or goggles to protect eyes.

• Wear a full length work apron and closed shoes to protect clothing and feet.

• Wear gloves when transporting larger sheets of glass. Carry glass in a vertical position with one hand supporting the sheet from below and the other hand steadying the sheet from the side.

• Use the proper equipment for sandblasting to minimize dust exposure.

• Wear double-cartridge respirator with filters to screen out dust produced from sandblasting, when refilling the unit with abrasive, and when cleaning the abrasive and dust off projects after blasting.

• Protective overalls, boots, and industrial-strength rubber gloves are required when sandblasting in a large, walk-in booth. Wear a sandblasting hood equipped with a fresh-air supply and respirator system.

• Wear earplugs or earmuff-style hearing protectors when sandblasting.

• Rinse completed objects with clear, running water before removing and discarding the resist. This will help prevent dust from becoming airborne and the abrasive from scratching the glass surface.

Visit your local safety supply store for pertinent information on the appropriate safety gear, respirators, and filters used for sandblasting.

Materials	Tools
1 pattern copy	apron
newspaper	safety glasses
glass	utility knife and/or stencil knife
cutter oil	permanent fine-tipped marker
glass cleaner	cork-backed straightedge
resist	glass cutter
masking tape	running pliers
isopropyl alcohol	breaking/combination pliers
	carborundum stone or wet/dry
	sandpaper or glass grinder
	soft cloths
	carbon paper
	hard-tipped pen or pencil
	squeegee

Selecting the glass

The following glasses are suitable for sandblasting.

Clear float glass Choose a minimum thickness of ⅛ in (3mm) for cabinet door inserts and window panels; ¼ in (6mm) for room dividers suspended in wood frames; and ⅜ in (10mm) or thicker for free-standing dividers and weight-bearing tabletops.

Mirrored glass Sandblast on back side of mirror to remove silvering in areas not covered by resist, producing a clean, crisp image. Sandblast front surface and a double image will be reflected by mirror backing.

Art glass Use colored art glass instead of clear float glass for cabinet inserts and sandblast design images on the smoothest side of the art glass. Sandblasting on colored glass will produce a 2-tone effect. Using darker colored sheets of glass will create dramatic contrasts between the clear and sandblasted areas.

Flashed glass This handblown antique glass has a thin layer of colored glass on top of a thicker, contrasting base color. When portions of top layer are sandblasted away, base coat is revealed in contrasting detail.

Tempered glass is float glass that has gone through a special heat treatment to increase its safety and durability. The process strengthens the sheet while creating a tension within the glass that, if broken, causes it to shatter into thousands of small pieces instead of larger, more dangerous shards. If your sandblasting project will be located in a high traffic area, verify if tempered glass is required by the local building and safety code before you begin. Tempered glass is difficult to sandblast without breaking it and is not recommended for hobbyists.

Glassware Decorate any piece of glassware with a sandblasted motif as long as the surface of the object is smooth enough for the resist to adhere to it and the glass is at least ⅛ in (3mm) thick. Popular glass items for sandblasting are vases, bowls, bottles, glasses, plates, and decanters.

Preparing the glass

Proper preparation of the glass to be sandblasted will ensure a successful project.

1 If the glass is scratched outside the area to be sandblasted, replace the glass with an unmarked piece or alter the design so that the mark is within the area to be sandblasted.

2 Cut and grind the glass to the required size and shape to fit within the pattern lines. When ordering float glass or mirror to a particular size and shape, have the edges swiped to remove the sharpness for safer handling.

3 Clean the surface thoroughly with a commercial glass cleaner or wash in warm, soapy water, rinse well and dry with a soft, lint-free cloth so that the resist will adhere firmly to the glass during cutting or sandblasting.

NOTE To prevent damage to the silvering, wipe the back of mirrors only if necessary. Use isopropyl alcohol or wash with warm water and a mild liquid soap.

Resist materials

The type of resist used is determined by the type of design and the sandblasting effect that is desired and by the surface being covered. Each project will list the type and thickness of resist recommended.

Vinyl sandblast resist   Available in rolls or sheets, usually in 4 mil, 6 mil, or 8 mil thicknesses (mil = thousandths of an inch). We recommend using 6 mil or 8 mil. Usually clear or opaque white, the vinyl has a thin layer of acrylic adhesive on the underside that is protected by a removable wax paper backing. After sandblasting, the adhesive pulls away cleanly from the glass surface. It is best used on flat or slightly curved surfaces.

Rubber sandblast resist   Stronger, more flexible, and conforms better to irregular surfaces. It is good for sandcarving images deep into the glass and works well on glassware and 3-dimensional objects. It comes in rolls or sheets with an adhesive backing.

Masking tape   Used to protect the underside of the glass from sandblasting grit. It can be substituted for resist (use a thicker masking tape designed for the automotive industry and sandblasting, and apply at least 2 or 3 overlapping layers). Masking tape usually does not produce as clean an edge along the cut line as resist and will dull the blades of the cutting knife faster.

Other materials   Use a number of pre-cut stencils or stencils created from materials found around the home or workshop. For freehand designs, apply beads of glue onto the glass with a hot glue gun. Use stickers, lettering, and labels of different sizes and shapes. Lace, cheesecloth, and loosely woven fabrics can be soaked in a mixture of glue and water, then pressed to the glass surface. Once dry, the object is sandblasted and the fabric removed to reveal a beautiful pattern.

Applying the resist

Make sure the work surface is clean and free of glass chips and debris. Cover the work surface with a towel or piece of carpeting and place the sheet of glass on top. If the resist being used is opaque, mask off the underside of the glass with overlapping rows of masking tape to prevent scratches.

1   Use a utility knife or scissors to cut a piece of resist paper approximately $\frac{1}{4}$ in to $\frac{1}{2}$ in wider on all sides than the piece of glass being prepared for sandblasting.

2   Separate approximately 1 in of the wax paper backing from one end of the resist and fold the paper back.

3   Center the resist over the glass and lay down with paper backing against glass. Verify that the resist is positioned properly and press exposed adhesive firmly to glass.

4   Work from right to left (reverse for left-handed) for ease in applying the resist. Position glass so the edge with the vinyl stuck to it is on the right-hand side. Place left hand under the resist and grasp the folded edge of the wax paper backing.

5   Peel away the paper backing with your left hand while using a squeegee in your right hand to adhere the resist to the

Center resist over glass, adhesive side down.
Press exposed adhesive to glass.

Peel back wax paper backing as resist is adhered to glass. Pull squeegee towards you in firm, downward motion.

Carefully puncture air bubbles with point of blade. Excessive pressure may scratch glass. Use squeegee to force air out through hole.

NOTE An opaque or overhead projector can be used to project larger designs onto the resist-covered glass. Use as a guideline only because the pattern image may be distorted when projected and enlarged. The pattern must be traced or photocopied onto a clear acetate film that can then be used to project the image onto the resist. Use a pencil to trace the design onto the resist. Make any alterations or adjustments required and trace over the pencil lines with a marking pen.

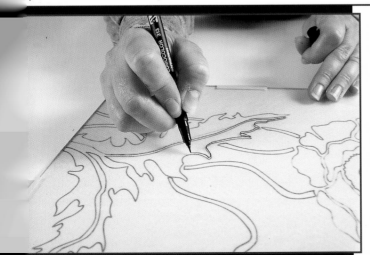

Lay glass covered with clear resist over pattern and trace design onto resist.

glass. Start at the top of the glass and pull the squeegee towards you in one firm downward sweeping motion (burnishing). Do not pull away the paper backing faster than the resist can be pressed to the glass or air bubbles will become trapped between the resist and the glass. The abrasive could tear through the resist, blasting the glass beneath.

6 Pierce a small hole in the resist with the point of the knife blade if some air bubbles are present. Do not scratch the glass beneath. Release the trapped air by pushing it out through the hole with your thumb or the squeegee. Place a small piece of resist or masking tape over the hole to keep out the abrasive. Air bubbles that are a few inches away from the area being sandblasted are not as much of a concern and can be left untouched if care is taken and the stream of abrasive is not aimed in that direction.

7 Turn the glass over and trim away the excess resist that is overlapping the edges.

Transferring the pattern onto the resist

The sandblasting patterns in this book are **block** designs (the easiest for single stage sandblasting) that can be adapted or altered to fit any size project. A block design is like a stencil, composed of individual design elements grouped together to form a pattern with a delineated space around each pattern element. How the design is transferred onto the resist is determined by whether the resist is clear or opaque.

Clear

1 Position the sheet of glass (with the resist-covered side facing upward) on top of the pattern copy that is taped to the work surface. Align with pattern.

2 Secure the glass to the pattern with masking tape.

3 Use a permanent fine-tipped marking pen to trace the pattern design onto the resist.

4 Remove the pattern. Cover the underside of the glass with overlapping rows of masking tape to prevent scratches and sandblasting abrasion. Trim away any masking tape that extends past the edge of the glass.

Opaque

For designs or sections of patterns that are 8½ in x 11 in or smaller

1 Cut a piece of carbon paper to fit the outline of the glass piece (or the pattern section) being sandblasted and tape to the opaque resist adhered to the glass surface.

2 Align the pattern copy over the carbon and secure in position with masking tape.

3 Using a hard-tipped pen, press firmly to trace design lines onto resist.

4 Remove the pattern copy and the carbon paper.

5 Trace over carbon lines with a permanent fine-tipped marker.

For larger sandblasting projects

1 Trim away excess paper around outside border of the pattern.

2 Align outside edges of pattern with edges of the glass sheet;

secure with masking tape.

3 Put carbon sheet between pattern and resist and trace design, one section at a time.

4 Remove the pattern and carbon paper. Trace over the carbon lines with the marking pen.

Cutting the resist

Cutting the resist accurately determines the overall appearance of any sandblasting project. Use a good stencil or utility knife with snap-off blades that are held firmly in place and do not flex or move within the handle. Have a supply of fresh blades on hand, and change the blade often. Discard blades in a small puncture-resistant container.

1 Before cutting the resist, determine whether the design being sandblasted is to be a positive or negative image (**positive**—design is sandblasted and background is clear; **negative**—background is sandblasted and image is clear).

2 Working from left to right (opposite for left-handed), begin cutting out the first pattern shape.

• Hold the knife (in your writing hand) like a pencil with your hand resting on the glass surface. The knife should be perpendicular to the glass and angled backwards slightly, not balanced on its point. Use your opposite hand to hold the glass steady.

• Cut the resist by pulling the blade in a smooth and flowing motion along the outline of the pattern shape. Use only enough pressure to cut the resist. Pressing too hard may score the glass surface.

• Try not to lift the blade from the resist until the entire outline of the shape has been cut. When cutting around shape perimeter, take care to have the end of the cut line meet precisely with the starting point. The juncture of these two points should not be visible.

• Do not cut past the pattern outline and into a section that is not being sandblasted. To do so may result in the blade leaving a scratch or score line on the glass in the area that is to be left clear. If you do cut past pattern outline, cover the perforation in the resist with masking tape to prevent abrasive from blasting through or lifting off the resist.

• Use a cork-backed metal ruler to cut straight lines accurately.

3 Positive sandblasting   Remove each shape from the glass as it is cut by inserting the blade tip into the incision, lifting a corner of the resist, and peeling the piece away from the glass.

Negative sandblasting   Cut around every design shape before carefully peeling away the resist covering the background.

4 Check for any areas of resist that may have lifted from the glass and press them down.

5 Dampen a soft cloth with a small amount of isopropyl alcohol and gently wipe away any adhesive left on the glass surface to prevent uneven frosting.

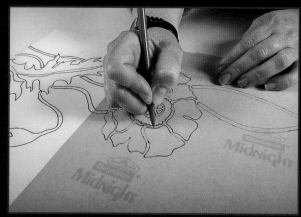

Designs can be transferred onto opaque resist and glass. Align pattern over carbon sheet on the resist-covered glass and trace design onto resist.

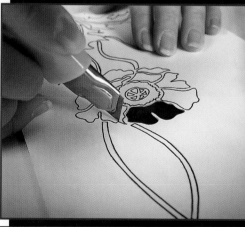

To cut resist, u[se?] a smooth and flowing pulling motion while drawing the kn[ife] blade along the outline of the pattern shape.

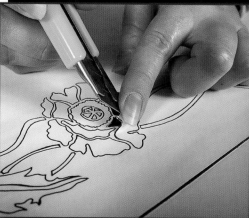

Insert blade tip into the cut pattern line, lif[t] and peel away resist to expose glass area to be sandblasted.

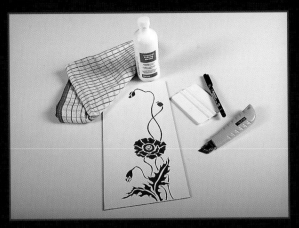

Use a small amount of alcohol on a soft cloth to remove any adhesive remaining on the glass surface.

Hold nozzle perpendicular to glass and approximately 6 to 8 in away from surface. Direct the spray of the abrasive across the glass surface in a continuous and overlapping back-and-forth motion.

Rinse glass with clean, warm water to prevent abrasive and glass dust from becoming airborne while removing resist. Wash glass with warm, soapy water and buff dry with a soft cloth.

Sandblasting the design

The glass piece is now ready for sandblasting. Most companies that offer sandblasting services charge a fee based on the number of pieces or by the hour. Or do the sandblasting yourself. Here's what's involved:

1 Place the glass piece in the sandblasting cabinet (see photo). Turn on the air compressor, ventilation system, and sandblasting equipment. When the air pressure is at the correct level, sandblasting can begin.

2 Place your hands into the protective gloves at the front of the booth and grasp the sandblasting nozzle with your writing hand. Turn on the supply of air and abrasive to the nozzle. If necessary, steady the glass with your opposite hand.

3 For successful sandblasting

• The nozzle should be perpendicular to the glass (not held at an angle) and approximately 6 to 8 in away from its surface.

  • Direct the spray of the abrasive (from the nozzle) across the front of the glass piece, using a slow and steady sweeping action. Do not point the nozzle and hold it in one position as the abrasive will carve into the glass and possibly blast through it or the adjacent resist.

  • Sandblast in a back-and-forth motion across the area to be frosted. Start at the top of the exposed glass, moving slowly towards the bottom with overlapping side-to-side passes. Extend the abrasive spray over the exposed area and onto the resist, at either end of each pass.

  • Make overlapping passes in an up-and-down motion from one side of the blasting area to the other to ensure even and complete coverage.

4 Turn off the equipment and wait for the dust in the cabinet to be cleared out by the ventilation system. Open the cabinet door and brush off any visible abrasive from the glass piece before removing it from the cabinet.

5 Inspect the glass for any uneven sandblasting. With a pencil, circle any areas requiring additional work and return to the cabinet for sandblasting. The pencil marks will be removed by the abrasive.

6 When the sandblasting is complete, rinse the glass piece under clean running water to remove abrasive and glass dust. This prevents particles from becoming airborne or scratching the glass surface once the resist is removed.

7 Peel off the resist and discard it.

8 Thoroughly clean the glass with warm, soapy water and then rinse with clean water. Buff dry with a soft, lint-free cloth to prevent the formation of water spots or streaks on the sandblasted areas. Do not use paper towels to clean or dry sandblasted glass. Use isopropyl alcohol to remove any stubborn adhesive and buff dry.

Sandblasting Projects & Patterns

29

Oriental Poppy

CABINET DOOR INSERT

Dimensions 13 in wide by 27 in high
Glass required 13 in x 27 in clear 3 mm float glass (per panel)
Resist recommended 14 in x 28 in clear 8 mil vinyl resist

To prepare the project for sandblasting, follow the instructions given for **How-to techniques** (pp22–28).

Special instructions

1 This pattern (p32) can be adapted to fit any size cabinet door and the design can be sandblasted to create either a positive or negative image. Reverse the pattern to provide a mirror image for a neighboring door, see photograph.

2 Decide whether the sandblasting will be on the front of the glass (facing into the room) or on the back side (interior of the cabinet). Keep in mind that the image will be reversed if the sandblasting is positioned so that it faces the interior of the cabinet. Reverse the pattern if necessary.

3 Before cutting the glass (pp15–19), measure the space where the glass is to be inserted from the back side of the cabinet door. Check the width and height of the opening in several locations for accuracy. The glass insert must be cut slightly smaller than the opening ($\frac{1}{16}$ in for each side of panel), to allow for ease of placement and for any deviations in the glass size or the cabinet opening. For example, the opening size in the cabinet door is $13\frac{1}{8}$ in wide by $27\frac{1}{8}$ in high; therefore, glass size is 13 in wide by 27 in high.

4 Take the sharpness off the edges of cut glass with a carborundum stone, wet/dry sandpaper, or a glass grinder (p20). Place the glass into the cabinet opening to verify the fit. If the corners of the cabinet opening are rounded, grind or groze the glass edges to fit.

Installing the cabinet door insert Glass inserts can be installed in a number of ways. If you do not have the skills or the tools to install the glass yourself, ask a friend or hire a professional.

1 Place door face down on work surface and position glass into opening.

2 Secure glass insert by using one of the following methods:

• Put a dab of silicone into each corner of door opening to prevent glass from rattling. Fasten appropriate length of wood molding to inside edges of cabinet door opening, with finishing nails. Use pre-cut wood moldings or make your own from material purchased at a local hardware or lumber store.

• Use small cabinet clips or turn buttons positioned along sides of opening to hold the glass firmly in place.

• Squeeze a bead of clear silicone caulking along the inside edge of the opening and into the allowance space between the insert and the sides of the opening. Allow to cure for 24 hours before moving or installing the door.

Positioning the sandblasted side towards the interior of the cabinet is preferable, especially in kitchens and other high traffic areas. Fingerprints and grime are easy to remove and less noticeable on the smooth side of the glass. In cabinets with interior lighting, the blasted image looks more spectacular and the illusion of depth is greater when backlit. However, in poor lighting conditions, the frosted areas may be more visible if the sandblasted image is on the front of the glass insert.

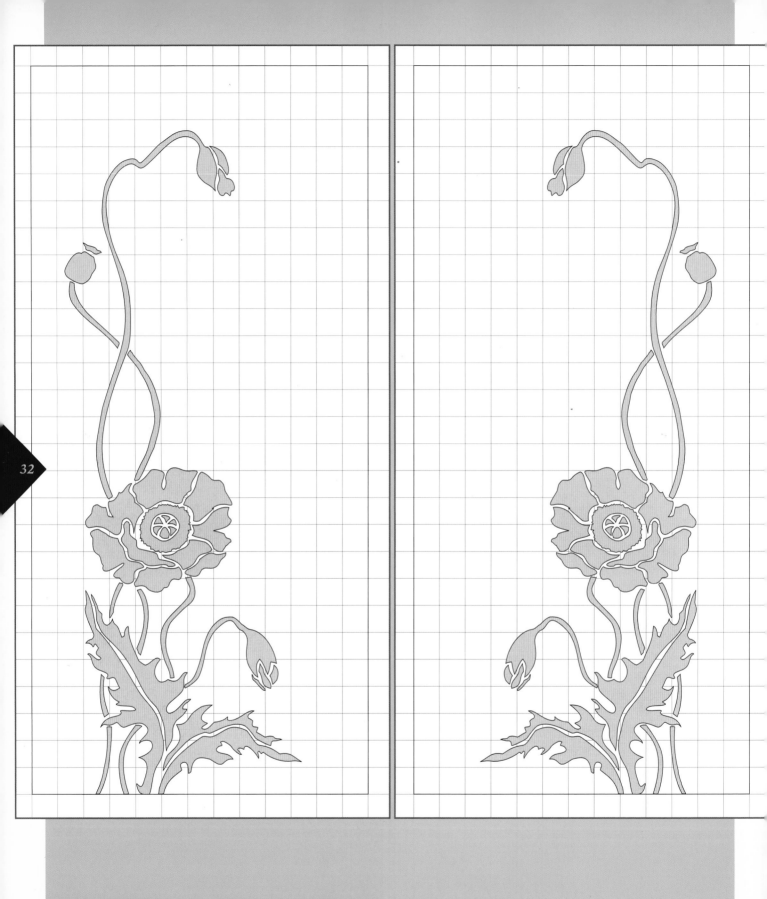

Falling Leaves
WALL MIRROR

Dimensions   18 in wide by 24 in high
Glass required   **A**   18 in x 24 in iridescent dark green
   B   15 in x 24 in 3 mm mirror
Resist recommended   19 in x 25 in opaque white or clear 8 mil resist for base piece
   30 in x 24 in opaque white or clear 8 mil resist for mirror overlay
Other materials   neutral curing silicone
   mirror clips

To prepare project for sandblasting, follow the instructions given for **How-to techniques** (pp22–28).

Special instructions
Base piece
1 Make irregular edge on base piece (A) of iridescent dark green art glass by nibbling away small bits of glass with grozing or combination pliers, or with a $\frac{1}{4}$ in grinding bit (p20). Rinse with clean running water and buff dry before applying resist to the iridescent side of the glass. Cover the underside of the glass with a single layer of overlapping rows of masking tape.

2 Cut the outline of each pattern shape before carefully removing the resist from the background of the glass. Press down and burnish any shape that may have lifted slightly from the glass surface.

3 Sandblast the background and along the irregular edge of the base piece. A negative image is created by sandblasting away the iridescent coating in the background while leaving the resist-covered design elements untouched. The strip of iridescence running through the middle represents the central vein of the mirrored leaf.

Leaf mirror overlay
1 Cut (pp15–19) the mirror into the 2 pattern shapes (B) (p34) that make up the halves of the mirrored leaf. Always cut mirrored glass on the glass side, not the silvered side. Smooth the sharp edges of the mirror with a carborundum stone, wet/dry sandpaper, or a glass grinder, taking care not to scratch the silver backing. Rinse and buff dry.

2 Protect the silvered side of the 2 mirror pieces with resist not masking tape. With a utility or stencil knife, trim away any excess resist that is overlapping the edges of the mirror. Turn the pieces over and repeat the process on the front.

3 Cut a slim, irregular line in the resist around the perimeter of each piece, on both the front and back sides of the mirror, and remove the resist along the edge.

4 Sandblast the outer edge on the front and back of each piece.

5 Rinse the mirror pieces under clean, running water and remove the resist. Buff dry.

Attaching the leaf mirror overlay to the base piece
1 Using the pattern as a guide, align the mirrored pieces along either side of the iridescent strip (representing the central vein of the leaf) located in the middle of the base piece. The iridescent vein should be

Sandblast to remove the iridescent coating in the background and to soften the irregular edges of the glass.

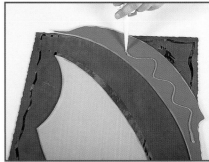

Adhere the leaf mirror overlay using neutral curing silicone. Align the two halves on each side of the iridescent strip (representing the vein of the leaf) that runs through the base piece.

visible through the gap between the 2 pieces of mirror. Check for correct alignment.

2 Remove one of the mirrored pieces from the base glass. Turn the mirror over and place a bead of silicone onto the center of the silvered side, and away from the outside edges, see photo (p33).

3 Turn the piece right side up and realign along the iridescent vein. Adhere the piece to the base, pressing firmly into position. Repeat with the second leaf overlay. Allow the silicone to cure (see manufacturer's instructions).

Installing the finished mirror

The mirror is fairly lightweight and can be hung on a wall with mirror clips.

> **Helpful hint** Use neutral curing silicone because it is noncorrosive and will not discolor or damage the silver backing on the mirror.

> NOTE To prevent damage to the silvering, wipe the back of mirrors only if necessary. Use isopropyl alcohol or wash with warm water and a mild liquid soap.

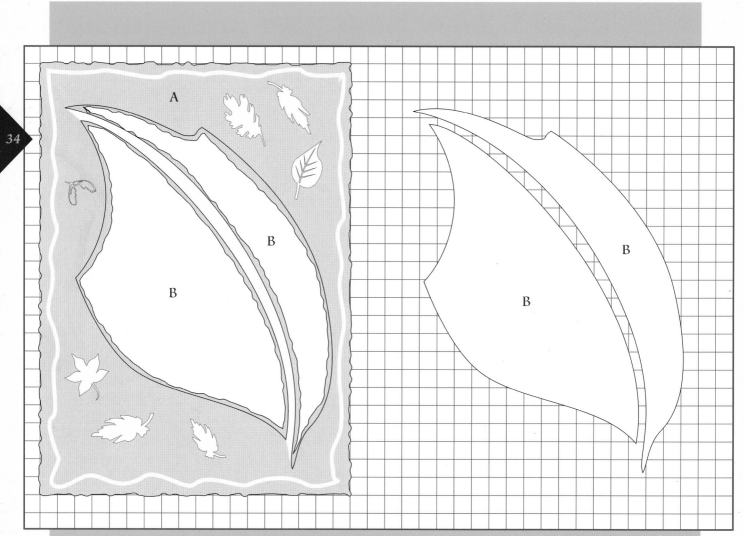

BACK PIECE WITH
TOP PIECES IN
POSITION

TOP PIECES

Elemental

CIRCULAR MIRROR

Dimensions 24 in diameter

Glass required 25 in x 25 in—$\frac{1}{8}$ in (3 mm) mirror

Resist recommended 25 in x 25 in clear or white 8 mil vinyl resist

Other materials cheesecloth

all-purpose white glue

mirror clips

To prepare the project for sandblasting, follow the instructions given for **How-to techniques** (pp22–28).

Special instructions

This mirror project (pattern, p38) can be adapted to accommodate any size. Use a purchased pre-cut mirror or have a mirror piece cut to order from a glass supplier and have the edges swiped to remove any sharpness. Or you can cut the glass yourself.

1 Cut mirrored glass on the glass side, not silvered side. See **Cutting circles, ovals, and outside curves** (p19) for cutting the circular shape.

2 Smooth any jagged edges (p20) along the perimeter of the mirror.

3 Moisten a piece of wet/dry sandpaper with water and rub it at a slight angle along the outside edges of the glass side of the mirror to remove any remaining sharpness. Rinse with clean, running water, and buff dry with a soft cloth.

4 The sandblasting will be done on the back of the mirror so apply the resist to the silvered side. Trim away the excess around the mirror's perimeter. Protect the glass side of the mirror with a single layer of overlapping rows of masking tape.

5 Transfer the design onto the resist (p26). The central circle of mirror that will not be sandblasted is 17 in in diameter with a $3\frac{1}{2}$ in border around the perimeter.

6 Using a utility or stencil knife, cut the outline of the central circle. Remove the resist from the border and press down and burnish the edges of the central circle of resist.

7 Mix $\frac{2}{3}$ cup of all-purpose white glue with $\frac{1}{3}$ cup of water in bowl. Immerse a piece of cheesecloth (larger than the mirror) in the glue mixture and let it soak for 2 to 3 minutes.

8 Cover the work surface with newspaper. Place the mirror on the work surface with the resist-covered silvering facing upward. Remove cheesecloth from the glue mixture and squeeze out some of the moisture. Drape over the entire mirror. For an interesting effect, twirl and rip holes in the cheesecloth fibers (within the border section) to create interesting patterns.

9 Allow cheesecloth to dry overnight until the moisture has evaporated. The cheesecloth should be stiff and firmly glued to the mirror.

10 Sandblast the border around the perimeter of the mirror, using less air pressure because the cheesecloth is not as strong as most

Soak cheesecloth in glue mixture before applying to mirror.

Lay cheesecloth over the silvered side of the mirror. Cover the entire surface.

Twirl and tear cheesecloth fibers to create organic patterns. Cheesecloth must be completely dry before sandblasting.

36

resist materials. A negative image will be created by sandblasting away the silver coating of the mirror while leaving the resist-covered circle untouched.

11 Rinse the mirror under warm, running water. Peel away cheesecloth, resist, and masking tape. Buff dry. Fasten mirror to wall with mirror clips.

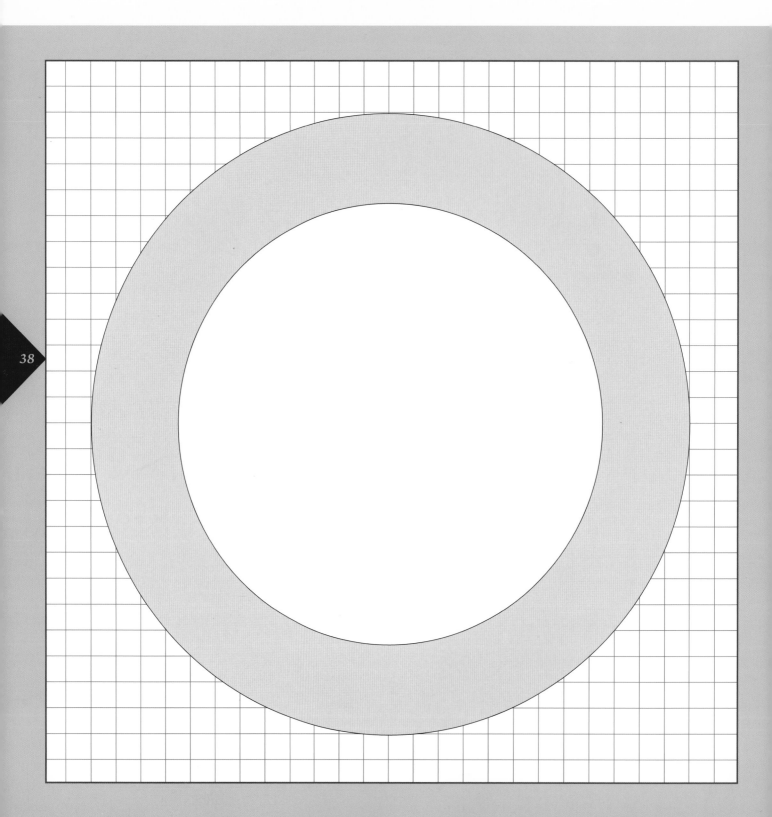

Prairie Harvest

DOOR AND SIDELIGHT INSERTS

Door insert
Dimensions   20 in wide by 64 in high
Glass required   20 in x 64 in—¼ in (6 mm) clear float glass
Resist recommended   21 in x 65 in clear 8 mil vinyl resist
Sidelight insert
Dimensions   7 in wide by 64 in high
Glass required   7 in x 64 in—¼ in (6 mm) clear float glass
Resist recommended   8 in x 65 in clear 8 mil vinyl resist

To prepare the project for sandblasting, follow the instructions given for **How-to techniques** (pp22–28).

Special instructions

1 These patterns (p40) can be adapted or reversed to fit any size door or sidelight and can also be used for inserts for cabinet or french doors. For more privacy, the background of this project has been sandblasted, resulting in a negative (clear) image. The design is also suitable for use as a positive image.

2 Purchase the glass for the door panel and sidelight inserts from a local glass supplier. Order the pieces cut to the required sizes and have the edges swiped to remove sharp edges. Wear protective gloves when handling or transporting large sheets of glass.

Installing the inserts

The sandblasted glass inserts installation depends on the location and type of door or sidelight unit. The inserts for our project are installed onto a standard exterior steel door unit containing triple pane sealed units suited for cold winters. The inserts are slightly larger than the sealed glass units and are secured to the door and sidelight using wooden corner moldings. An air space is created between the sealed unit and the glass insert, adding further insulation value and preventing moisture buildup between the 2 glass surfaces. Brass wood screws are used to fasten the corner moldings to the moldings that hold the sealed units in place (see photo). To deter the inserts from rattling within the framework, place several dabs of silicone along the inside of the moldings before securing the glass in place. The glass inserts have been positioned so that the sandblasted side is facing inward, towards the sealed units. In high traffic areas this is important to prevent fingerprints and dirt from marring the sandblasted areas.

Secure the glass inserts to the door and sidelight with corner moldings and brass screws. For easy cleaning, position the sandblasted side of the glass towards the sealed unit.

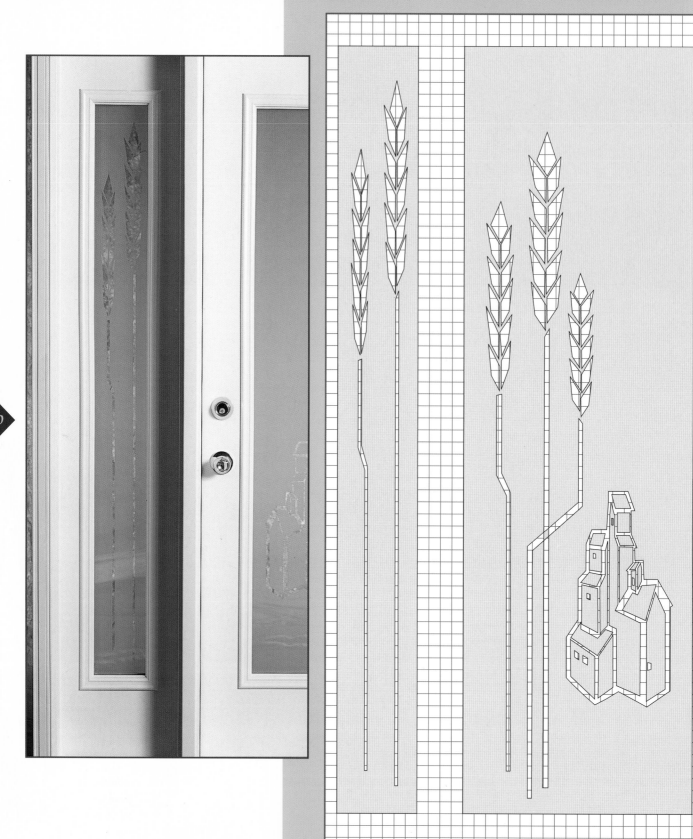

Safari

COFFEE TABLE

Dimensions   18 in wide by 48 in long by 16½ in high
Glass required   1 piece 18 in x 48 in x ½ in (12 mm) clear float glass for tabletop
4 pieces 10 in x 16 in x ⅜ in (10 mm) clear float glass for pedestals
Resist recommended   2 pieces of 19 in x 49 in clear 8 mil vinyl resist
Other materials   4 — 90° 2-way chrome furniture connectors for ⅜ in glass
40 in length of clear heavy glasstop vinyl molding for ⅜ in glass

To prepare the project for sandblasting, follow the instructions given for **How-to techniques** (pp22–28).

Special instructions

Purchase the glass for the tabletop (pattern, p44) and pedestals from a local glass supplier. Order the pieces cut to the required sizes and have the edges seamed to remove sharp edges. You may wish to have the corners of the tabletop piece slightly rounded. Wear protective gloves when handling or transporting large sheets of glass.

Tabletop   The glass tabletop weighs approximately 40 pounds and you may require assistance during various sandblasting and assembling stages.

1 Apply clear resist to both sides of tabletop. Burnish tightly to the glass. Trim overlap.

2 Transfer the zebra pelt pattern to the resist. On the same side, measure and mark a 1 in border around the perimeter of the tabletop using a straightedge and marker. The design is sandblasted as a positive image and the background is left clear. A sandblasted border surrounds the edges of the tabletop and overlaps onto the top and the underside of the glass. The border provides a graphic frame for the central design as well as acting as a visual reminder of the location of the table edges.

3 Use a utility or stencil knife to cut around the pattern outline of each design shape and remove the resist from each piece as it is cut. Using a straightedge as a guide, cut and remove the resist around the 1 in wide border on this side of the glass.

4 Turn the tabletop over and proceed to measure, cut, and remove the resist from the ½ in border that is to be sandblasted on this side.

5 Sandblast both sides and the edges of the tabletop. Create additional interest by sandblasting the zebra pattern a bit deeper (also known as sandcarving) into the glass.

Pedestals   The tabletop is supported by a glass pedestal at either end, each made of 2 pieces of ⅜ in (10 mm) thick glass, and held together at right angles by a pair of glass furniture connectors.

1 Sandblast all sides and edges of the 4 pieces of ⅜ in float glass. Rinse with warm, running water and buff dry.

2 Form a pedestal by clamping 2 of the glass pieces together at a 90° angle with a pair of furniture connectors attached 2 in from the top and bottom edges of the glass. Tighten the set screws which should have nylon tips to prevent chipping the glass. If they do not, insert small felt or rubber bumper pads between the ends of the screws and the glass.

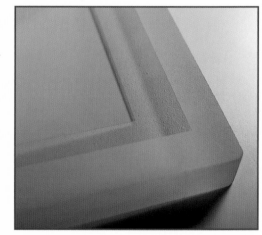

A border has been sandblasted on the top and bottom sides of the tabletop to create depth and to frame the zebra pattern.

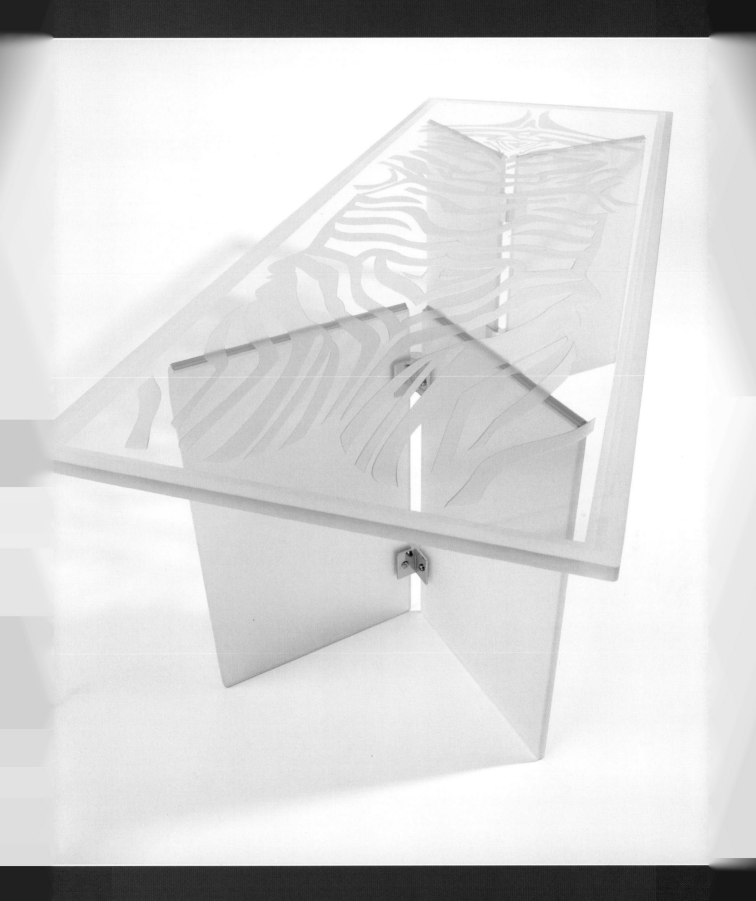

3 Cut the length of clear vinyl molding into 4—10 in pieces with a utility knife. Fit the molding over the top edges of the glass pedestals to act as a cushion between the pedestals and the glass tabletop. If this molding is not available, use clear plastic desk buttons.

Assembling the table

1 Align the pedestals approximately 22 in apart, with the clamped ends facing each other.

2 Center the tabletop over the pedestals with the zebra pelt design on the underside of the glass.

Option Create a different look by reversing areas to be sandblasted.

• Produce a negative image by leaving the zebra pelt clear and sandblasting the entire background.

• For a more subtle look, leave the pedestal glass clear and eliminate the sandblasted border around the perimeter of the tabletop. Extend the design lines of the zebra pelt so that the expanded pattern fills the underside of the tabletop. When ordering the glass pieces, have the edges polished or beveled for a clean, crisp look.

Apply clear heavy glasstop vinyl molding to the top edges of each pedestal to act as a cushion and to help hold the tabletop in position.

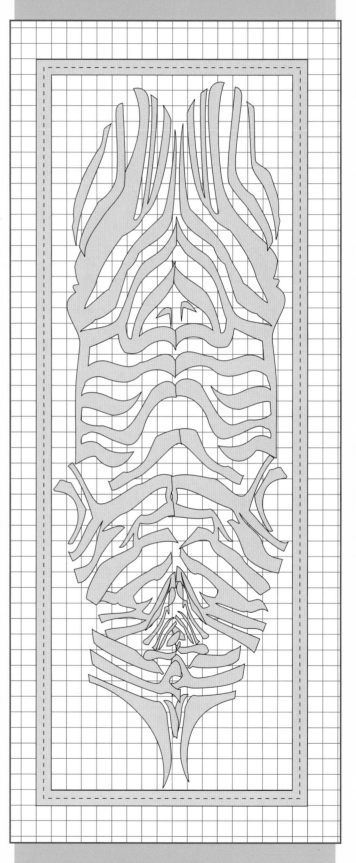

Oceana

ACCENT TABLE

Dimensions   24 in wide by 34 in long by 32½ in high
Glass required   1 piece 26 in x 36 in x ⅜ in (10 mm) clear float glass for tabletop
  3 pieces 14 in x 32 in x ⅜ in (10 mm) clear float glass for pedestal
Resist recommended   2 pieces of 24 in by 34 in clear 8 mil vinyl resist
Other materials   2 — 120° 3-way chrome furniture connectors for ⅜ in glass
  33 in length of clear heavy glasstop vinyl molding for ⅜ in glass

To prepare the project for sandblasting, follow the instructions given for **How-to techniques** (pp22–28).

Special instructions

Purchase the ⅜ in (10 mm) clear float glass for the tabletop (pattern, p46) and pedestal from a local glass supplier. Because of the thickness and irregular shape of this glass table, you will need heavy-duty breaking and running pliers designed for thicker glass to break out the score lines (pp15–19) necessary to achieve the pattern outline. Or make a cardboard template of the tabletop, then order the glass pieces cut to the required size and shape, and have the edges swiped. Because of their larger size, you may require assistance during various sandblasting and assembly stages.

Tabletop   Details are sandblasted onto top and underside of the tabletop. The edges of the glass are chipped away to create an irregular and jagged edge. (If you do not want the jagged edge, cut the resist to the border design as indicated on the pattern and sandblast the perimeter of the tabletop). Once the tabletop has been cut to the pattern outline, the edges of the glass must be chipped to produce the jagged edge. Practice chipping a piece of scrap glass before starting on the tabletop.

1   Lay the glass on the work surface with one side overhanging the edge. Put a piece of carpet or a thick towel underneath the glass. Place a large plastic or metal container below the extending glass to catch the glass fragments.

2   Hold the glass against the work surface with one hand, and begin chipping away at the edge of the glass with a pair of grozing or combination pliers. Position the jaws of the pliers about ¼ in from the edge, grip firmly, and begin breaking away fragments of glass. Use a combination of upward and downward motions and exert a fair amount of pressure to produce a jagged edge around the tabletop.

3   Brush the glass fragments from the tabletop and work surface with a bench brush and dust pan. Sweep the entire work area and place the glass chips in a puncture-resistant container.

4   Clean the glass tabletop with soap and water and wipe dry. Apply the clear resist to both sides of the tabletop and burnish tightly to the glass. Trim away overlap.

5   Transfer designs for top and underside of tabletop to resist. As well as a central motif, a sandblasted border surrounds the edges of the tabletop and overlaps onto the top and the underside of the glass.

6   Cut around the pattern outline of each design shape with the utility or stencil knife and remove each piece of resist as it is cut. Repeat on both sides of tabletop.

7   Sandblast both sides and the edges of the tabletop. Create a dramatic effect by

Detail of tabletop edge.

Safety precautions

• Always wear safety glasses, a work apron, and a pair of protective gloves. when chipping the edges of glass.
• Use a plastic or metal container to catch glass fragments as they are broken away.
• Use a bench brush and dust pan to sweep chips from the main piece of glass and the work surface.
• When disposing of unwanted glass, place the discards in a thick-walled cardboard box that is puncture-resistant.

sandblasting a bit deeper into the glass (along the edge of the resist still remaining on the glass). Sandblast the perimeter enough to remove the sharpness and round off chipped areas that are thinner and more jagged than necessary.

Pedestal   The support structure for the tabletop is comprised of 3 pieces of sandblasted ⅜ in (10 mm) thick glass, held securely in position by a pair of glass furniture connectors.

8   Create a jagged finish along the curved outside edge of the 3 pedestal pieces by using the method described in steps 1 to 3.

9   Sandblast sides and edges on the 3 pieces of ⅜ in float glass. Rinse and buff dry.

10   To form the pedestal, clamp the glass pieces together at a 120° angle with a pair of furniture connectors approximately 3 to 4 in from the top and bottom edges of the glass and tighten the set screws. Screws should have nylon tips to prevent chipping the glass. If they do not, insert small felt or rubber bumper pads.

11   Cut the length of clear vinyl molding into 3—11 in pieces with a utility knife. Fit over top edges of each pedestal leg to act as a cushion between the pedestal and the glass tabletop. If this molding is not available, use clear plastic desk buttons.

Assembling the table   Center the tabletop over the pedestal with the central sandblasted motif on the underside of the glass. Place the glass top on the upright support structure.

Grozing or combination pliers can be used to produce a jagged edge. Use combination of upward and downward motions and exert a fair amount of pressure to chip away glass along the edge.

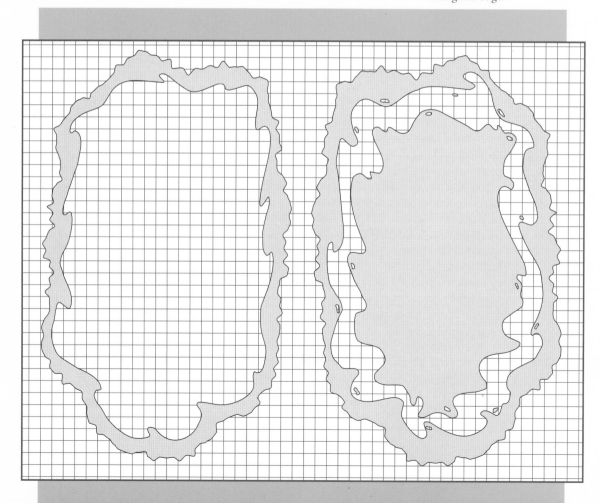

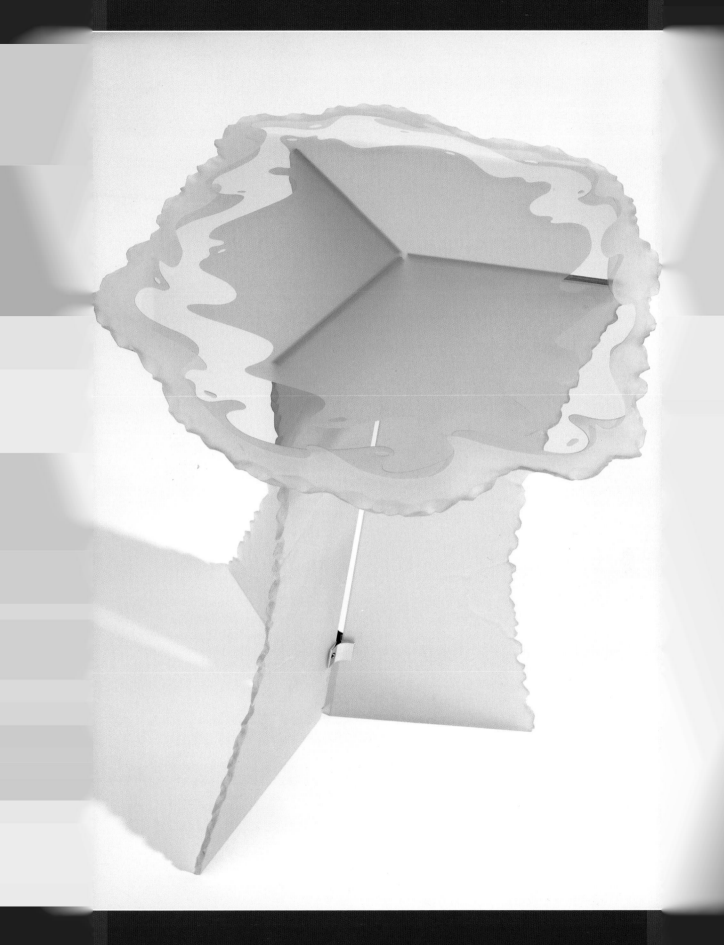

Glassware Ideas

Once you have taken up sandblasting, you will never look at a plain glass object the same way again. Almost any piece of glassware can be enhanced as long as the chosen object is at least ⅛ in (3 mm) thick and a resist material can stick to it. Many interesting effects can be achieved by employing a variety of materials as resist—lace, loosely woven fabrics such as cheesecloth, self-adhesive vinyl lettering (Letraset®), hot glue, etc. Create your own designs or look to design, stencil, or clip-art books and computer programs for inspiration. Here are just a few suggestions.

Pre-cut stencils   For quick and easy designs, use paint or quilt stencils as pattern templates. Cover area to be sandblasted with rubber or 8 mil vinyl resist. Cover glass not being sandblasted with heavy-duty masking tape. Trace the outlines of the images directly onto the resist and cut out the individual shapes. For positive sandblasting, remove each shape as it is cut. For negative blasting images, cut all the design shapes and then carefully remove the resist from the background.

Self-adhesive vinyl lettering (Letraset®)   Use self-adhesive vinyl lettering and shapes to jazz up ordinary glassware. Sandblast entire background or a select area can be chosen and the balance of the object masked off. To prevent sandblast abrasive from marking the inside of a glass object with a wide opening, fill the glass with crushed tissue paper or newspaper and hold in place with masking tape. Place the glass upside down on the work surface and trim away the excess tape that is overlapping the rim of the glass. If a clear rim is desired, align the straight edge of a strip of masking tape along the lip of the glass and press the overlap onto the masking tape covering the top opening. Press the desired vinyl lettering and shapes onto the glass surface and burnish well. Mask off any other areas that are to remain clear and proceed to sandblast the exterior.

Hot glue   Hot glue can be used to "draw" freeform designs onto the glass and to act as the resist material. Once the object has been sandblasted, rinse the abrasive off with warm water and pick off glue.

Lace and loosely woven fabrics   Lace, cheesecloth, crotcheted doilies, etc. can make interesting images for sandblasting. Simply mask off any area that is to be left untouched, leaving areas to be sandblasted exposed. Allow the material to soak in a solution of 2 parts all purpose white glue and one part water for a few minutes. Remove the material, gently squeeze out the excess moisture, drape material onto the desired area and press gently to the glass surface. Allow to dry overnight. Once sandblasted, soak in warm water to loosen the material from the object's surface.

Clip-art and design books and computer programs   Thousands of images in clip-art and design books and computer programs are available to decorate objects.

"Draw" free-form designs with a hot glue gun. Use vinyl lettering to personalize glassware.

Soak lace in a mixture of glue and water and adhere to glass surface. Sand-blasting will impart the intricate details of the lace onto the glass.

Helpful hint Always test any type of alternate resist material on an inexpensive or scrap piece first. For some materials that may not be as durable as sandblasting resist, the amount of air pressure may have to be decreased.

Helpful hint When it doesn't matter whether the object is sandblasted in the positive or the negative, get 2 uses from one piece of resist. Cover one object with resist and trace the chosen pattern onto it. As each shape is cut and removed from the glass, place the resist cutouts onto a second glass object and burnish to the surface. When the glass is sandblasted, two different looks from the same pattern shapes are the result—one positive and one negative. Wine bottles are ideal for this method.

49

Stained Glass

Selecting glass

The combination of color, texture, and light plays a major role in determining how successful the outcome of a stained glass piece will be. Take your time when choosing glass, enjoy the process, and keep the following guidelines in mind:

• View glass selections in lighting conditions similar to those where the finished project will be displayed. For pieces that will not be backlit or transmitting light, select glasses that are attractive in reflective light or lighter in color.

• Try to keep color selections to a minimum. Larger projects can use more color variations: small projects, use 2 or 3 colors. For variety, try using varying shades or textures of one of the dominant colors. View glass choices side by side to see how the colors affect each other; soften with lighter colors and clear textured glasses.

• Consider the use of your stained glass project—decorative, functional, creating privacy?

• Opalescent glass for a lamp shade can disguise the electrical components and soften light bulb glare. Textured glasses or sandblasting the lamp shade interior are interesting alternatives.

Leaded glass construction

Lead came is the traditional material used to join and hold together pieces of glass to form a stained glass panel. The term "leaded glass" refers to this centuries-old method. Lead is an inexpensive and flexible metal that can be cut easily and bent around glass pieces that have curving lines. Zinc, brass, and copper cames are more rigid and harder to cut and bend. They are used for border cames and larger panels that require more support and have straight or only slightly curving design lines.

Came comes in 6 ft lengths and a variety of widths in H-shaped and U-shaped profiles. A length of came has 3 components—leaf (face), heart, and channel. The **leaf** is the surface on either side of the came that overlaps the edges of the glass and is left exposed once the panel has been assembled. It has either a flat or a rounded profile and its width is the measurement given when a came size is listed. The **channel** runs the length of the came. H-shaped came has 2 back-to-back channels that hold adjoining glass pieces in position on the interior of a stained glass panel. It can also be used as a border came in certain situations. U-shaped came has only one channel and is used as a border around the perimeter of panels. The **heart** is the part of the came that the glass pieces rest against inside the channel. The width of lead came pattern lines is usually $1/16$ in and allows for the thickness of the came's heart to fit between the adjoining pieces of glass. The height of the heart is fairly standard and will accommodate the thickness of most art glasses. For glasses that are heavily textured or thicker, cames are available with a higher heart.

Stained glass panels constructed with lead came are assembled in a particular sequence:

• Draw a pattern to the correct scale: make 2 or 3 accurate copies.

Please review **Safety guidelines**, p13, before working with lead.

• Cut required glass pieces, using the pattern as a guide.

• Tape a copy of the pattern to a wood board or work surface, and line up and fasten wood trim along one side and one end of the pattern's perimeter.

• Cut outside border cames to the appropriate length, and align an end and side piece on the pattern adjacent to the 2 pieces of wood trim.

• Assemble glass pieces on the pattern, starting at the corner where the 2 pieces of border came meet. Grind to fit if necessary and secure in place with pieces of lead came and horseshoe nails.

• Put the 2 remaining border cames in place and solder together each juncture where 2 or more pieces of came meet.

• Cement, clean, and reinforce panel as necessary.

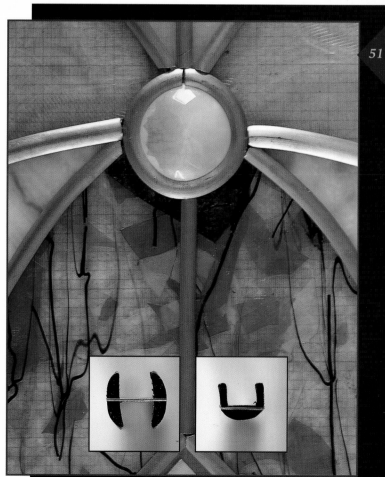

At left, H-channel came; at right, U-channel came. Background photo shows the use of H- channel cames.

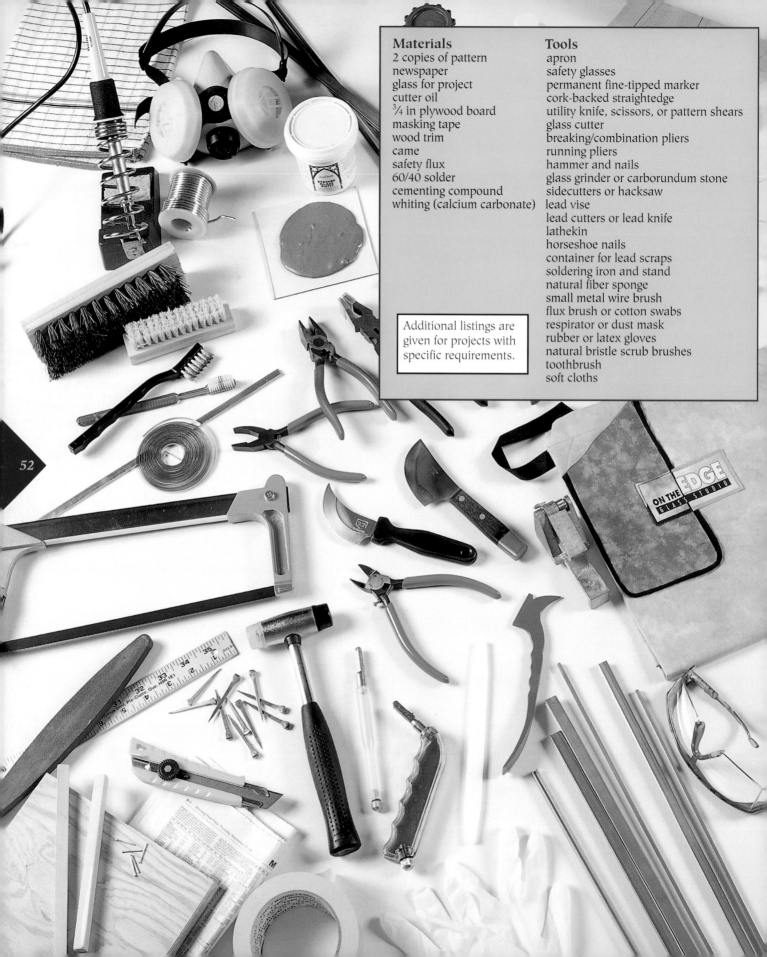

Materials
2 copies of pattern
newspaper
glass for project
cutter oil
¾ in plywood board
masking tape
wood trim
came
safety flux
60/40 solder
cementing compound
whiting (calcium carbonate)

Tools
apron
safety glasses
permanent fine-tipped marker
cork-backed straightedge
utility knife, scissors, or pattern shears
glass cutter
breaking/combination pliers
running pliers
hammer and nails
glass grinder or carborundum stone
sidecutters or hacksaw
lead vise
lead cutters or lead knife
lathekin
horseshoe nails
container for lead scraps
soldering iron and stand
natural fiber sponge
small metal wire brush
flux brush or cotton swabs
respirator or dust mask
rubber or latex gloves
natural bristle scrub brushes
toothbrush
soft cloths

Additional listings are given for projects with specific requirements.

52

How-to techniques

Refer to **Basic techniques** (pp14–20) for detailed instructions on making copies of the patterns, cutting the glass pieces, and smoothing or grinding glass edges.

Preparing the pattern   Each lead came pattern in this book has **perimeter lines** that determine the overall dimensions of the panel and **cutting lines** that define the outermost edges to which the glass pieces are cut and fit. **Pattern lines** outline the shape of each individual glass piece and represent the space to allow between pieces to fit the lead came.

To draw an accurate pattern for lead came construction

1 Use a straightedge and permanent fine-tipped marker to measure and draw the **perimeter lines** onto a piece of drawing vellum (drafting vellum or graph paper divided into grids). Verify corners with a drawing square.

2 Measure and draw **cutting lines** within the perimeter lines. Cutting lines have been marked on each pattern but may need adjusting for came size and depth of the channels. Use method A or B for precise **cutting lines**:

A Align a small length of border came along the inside edge of the perimeter line. Insert a straightedge into the came's channel, pressing it firmly against the heart of the came with a portion of the straightedge extending past either end. Use a pencil to mark points along the length of the straightedge closest to the perimeter line. Once connected, these points will form a cutting line. Use this method to create the cutting lines for each side of the pattern.

B Insert a straightedge into the border came's channel, pressing it firmly against the heart of the came. A portion of the straightedge must extend past one end of the came. With a ruler or measuring tape, measure the distance between the outermost edge of the border came and the side of the straightedge resting against the came's heart. Use that measurement to mark and draw in the cutting lines on the pattern.

3 Transfer the pattern lines onto the vellum, using one of the methods in **Making copies of the patterns** (p14). Use a pencil and stay within the outline of the cutting lines. If pre-cut bevels or jewels are required, verify that they fit or alter the pattern. When pattern lines are accurate, ink them in with a permanent fine-tipped marker line that will allow a $1/16$ in space for the thickness of the lead came's heart between each glass piece.

4 Make 2 or 3 copies of the pattern to use for cutting and assembling the stained glass panel.

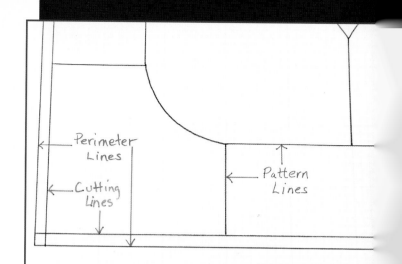

Take the time to draw an accurate pattern.

The depth of the border came channel determines the location of the cutting line.

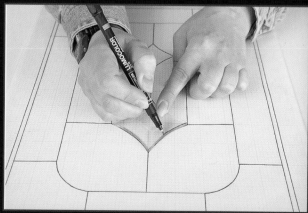

Verify that pre-cut bevels fit within the pattern lines. If necessary, adjust the pattern lines or grind bevel edges to fit.

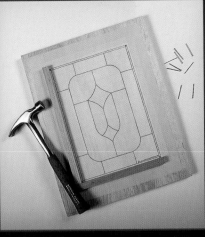

Helpful hint If stretched came channel is too narrow for glass pieces, insert the end of a lathekin into the channel until it rests against the heart and run it the length of the came to widen it.

Set up project board by aligning wood trim along perimeter line on one side and one end of the pattern.

Stretch lead came to straighten it and eliminate slack. Place one end in lead vise and use pliers to grasp and pull other end.

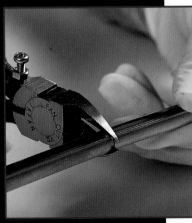

...d came by using an even
...e to rock knife back and
...ross came leaf.

With channel facing up, use lead cutters to cut lead in a scissor-like motion.

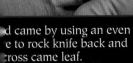

...elpful hint Sharpen lead knife frequently on a carborundum ...one. Place a few drops of lightweight machine oil on the top ...rface of the stone, hold blade parallel to the stone's surface, ...d use a circular motion to sharpen the blade. Sharpen both ...des of the knife's blade. Lead dykes do not wear as quickly and ...ould be taken to a professional tool-sharpener.

Preparing the project board

If you build the panel on a separate project board, nails can be driven into it and the project can be put away when the panel is not being worked on.

1 Use a piece of ¾ in thick plywood that is 3 to 4 in wider on each side than the stained glass panel (for a 10 in x 14 in panel, use 16 in x 20 in plywood board).

2 Tape a copy of pattern to project board. Do not tape over perimeter lines.

3 Assemble leaded glass windows by starting in a bottom corner (usually left for right-handed people) and working upwards and outwards. Align lengths of wood trim to just cover the perimeter lines of the side and end of the chosen corner of the pattern and nail into place.

Stretching lead came

Before use, lead came must be stretched to straighten it, remove kinks, and eliminate slack.

1 Lay length of came onto work surface, channel facing up. Untwist kinks.

2 Clamp one end of came into a lead vise fastened to the end of work surface.

3 Grasp the opposite end of the came with a pair of pliers and pull evenly until the lead is straight and firm. Use pliers with serrated jaws to prevent slipping. The lead should stretch several inches, becoming taut.

4 Handle the lead came carefully to prevent unwanted crimps and twists.

Cutting lead came

It is important to cut the lead came cleanly and evenly, without crushing the channels. Use lead came cutters or a traditional lead knife.

Lead cutters (also known as **lead dykes** or **knippers**) are fashioned like pliers with sharp, pointed jaws for straight or mitered angle cuts.

1 Mark lead came with a horseshoe nail or marker for position and angle of cut.

2 With channel facing up, cut the came using a scissor-like motion. Position the flat side of the lead cutters adjacent to the portion of the came being trimmed and away from the excess length being cut away.

3 To cut an acute angle, cut a piece of lead came to the maximum required length, snip out part of the came's heart, then individually trim the top and bottom leaves to the angle marked.

Lead knife has a sharp, curved blade with a short, weighted handle, that can be used to tamp pieces of glass into position inside the lead came channel.

1 Mark came's leaf with a horseshoe nail or marker at position and angle of cut.

2 Place came on a flat, level surface with leaf of came facing up, and align knife blade on cutting mark.

3 Rock knife back and forth using even, gentle pressure to make cut. Reopen came channel with lathekin, if needed.

Cutting zinc and other rigid metal cames

Zinc, brass, and copper cames are more rigid and do not require stretching. Use one of the following methods to cut these cames. Remove burrs with a small file.

Hacksaw Clamp one end of the came in a vice secured to the end of the work surface. The marked leaf (facing up) should protrude beyond the vise. Align the hacksaw's fine-toothed, metal-cutting blade on the marked angle and grasp the end of the came sticking out of the vise with your free hand. Saw through the metal came. If a vice is not available, use a miter box or have someone assist you.

Miter came saw Before operating this power tool, read and follow the manufacturer's instructions and safety guidelines. Set the saw blade at the required angle for the cut. Align the marked leaf of the came with the saw blade, clamp into position, and make the desired cut. Always wear safety glasses when operating power tools.

Sidecutters Use these (or lead cutters) to snip the leaf of the came and then gently bend the came back and forth until the heart snaps and the came is separated into 2 pieces.

Border cames

Lead, zinc, brass, or copper U-channel cames come in a variety of widths, provide a finished look, and are recommended for most free-hanging stained glass panels. Zinc U-channel is a popular choice, especially for square and rectangular panels. It is a strong, rigid material that is lightweight and similar in color to lead came. Stained glass panels that are to be installed into specifically-sized openings are often fitted with H-channeled lead came. This provides a slight allowance for error because if a panel is too large, the outer portion of the came's leaf can be cut away or shaved to fit into the opening. Lead is often preferred for architectural openings because of its malleability. The size and type of came recommended are listed for each project.

Free-hanging panels Cut a piece of U-channel border came for each side of the panel the exact measurement of the corresponding perimeter line. Miter each end of the came pieces at an inward 45° angle so that a 90° angle is formed when an end and a side piece are brought together. Because the entire panel will be visible when hung, mitering the came will produce neat corners with a finished appearance.

Architectural panels Border cames are often covered by framing materials when a stained glass panel is installed into an opening, so mitering the corners is not necessary. Cut the 2 side pieces of H-channel came the exact length of the side perimeter lines. The top and bottom border cames are cut the length of their corresponding perimeter lines minus the width of the border cames on either side. For example, a 34 in wide by 22 in high panel that is framed with came that has a ½ in leaf width, will have side cames that measure 22 in in length. The top and bottom cames will both be cut 33 in long to take into consideration the ½ in width of the came pieces on either side. Always cut the side came pieces the full length of the perimeter line to distribute some of the weight of the panel.

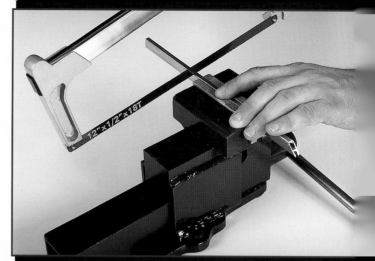

Clamp rigid metal came in a vise and use a hacksaw to cut at the prescribed mark.

NOTE The saw blade guard has been raised for photographic purposes.

A came saw is a fast and efficient way to cut rigid metal cames.

Snip came leaf on both sides of the heart. Bend the came back and forth until the heart snaps.

Below left: Cut U-channel zinc border came at a 45° angle to for a professional looking corner for free-hanging panels.

At right: H-channel lead came is often used for architectural pane borders. The outside came edges can be trimmed if necessary to into an opening. (Shown before corner has been soldered.)

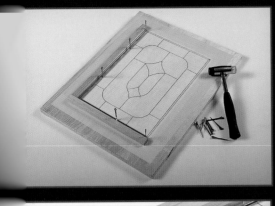

Hold border cames in place against wood trim with horseshoe nails.

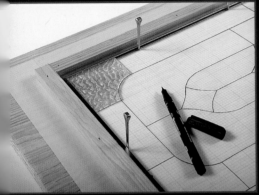

Insert the first piece of glass into the corner formed by the 2 border cames. Glass piece must fit within the pattern lines.

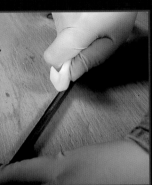

Use a lathekin to widen came channel to accept glass pieces of varying widths.

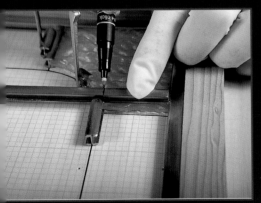

Mark position and angle to be cut on came leaf. Make allowance for overlapping leaf on adjacent and intersecting pattern lines.

Trim came to fit.

lways have a container on hand for
he safe storage of lead came scraps.

Leading the panel

1 Verify that the channels of the border came pieces are open and fit the width of the glass pieces (use a lathekin to open closed channels and file to remove burrs). Align border came pieces flush against the 2 strips of wood trim fastened to the project board along the perimeter lines. The abutting ends of the 2 cames must fit together accurately to form a right angle and the cames must be the correct length. Hold the border pieces in position by hammering in several horseshoe nails. The flat side of the nails must rest against the inside edge of the cames, trapping them between the wood trim and the nails. Secure a nail at the far end of each came so that it does not slide out of position. If possible, use a dual head glazing hammer that is light and has a hard plastic head for hammering nails and a softer rubber head for gently tapping glass pieces into lead came channels.

2 Insert the first piece of cut glass into the corner created by the 2 pieces of border came. If cut correctly, the glass piece should fit into the channels of both cames with the exposed edges of the glass fitting just inside the pattern lines. Mark any area of glass that overlaps the pattern lines and remove the excess by grinding or grozing. Slight discrepancies in size and shape will usually be covered by the leaf of the came. However, if the glass is smaller than it should be by a significant amount, re-cut the piece to the proper size so that the leading of the panel has a solid foundation on which to build.

3 Lead is malleable and conforms to curved or circular shapes but not around sharp corners. It must be cut to fit. Lead one pattern line at a time, beginning with a line that intersects with one of the border cames. Cut a manageable length of H-channel lead came, slightly longer than the pattern line. Place the came over the exposed edge of the glass piece and butt one end of it against the border came, conforming the lead to the shape of the glass and the pattern line. The end of the H-channel came may need to be angled to ensure a tight fit against the border came. Mark the came with a fine-tipped marker or the point of a horseshoe nail. Remove the came from the project board and trim to fit.

4 Butt the trimmed end of the came against the border came. The opposite end of the came must be cut slightly shorter than the pattern line to accommodate the overlapping leaf of the came that will be fitted along the nearest intersecting pattern line. Fit a scrap of the type of came that will be used on the intersecting pattern line onto the edge of the glass piece already in place. Remove the scrap after using a marker to draw a line onto the glass along the outside edge of the overlapping leaf of the came. Mark and trim the piece of came being fitted to the length and angle marked on the glass. Measure and cut accurately. (See photo.)

5 Cut lengths of H-channel came to fit each of the pattern lines that surround the glass piece being fitted. Avoid gaps between abutting pieces.

6 While leading the panel, glass pieces and fitted lengths of came must be anchored so that they do not shift out of position. Situate small scraps of lead came (at least ½ to 1 in long) up against fitted lengths of came and along glass edges, and secure them in their correct positions by hammering in horseshoe nails, with the flat side of each nail fixed tightly against the lead scrap. To prevent chips along the glass edge and nail indentations on the lead came, always insert lead scraps between the horseshoe nails and the pieces being secured.

7 Fit remaining glass pieces and lead cames in the same way. Each piece fitted should provide support and a base upon which to assemble successive pieces.

8 Remove the horseshoe nails and the pieces of scrap lead from one panel edge at a time and carefully slip on the corresponding border cames without dislodging the glass pieces or the fitted H-channel pieces. The border cames should align with the inner edge of the perimeter line of the pattern. Secure in position using lead scraps and horseshoe nails once you are satisfied that the corners are square and the border cames are in position.

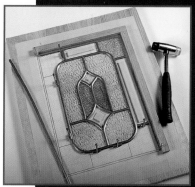

Use horseshoe nails and lead scraps to anchor glass and came pieces in position.

Secure remaining 2 border cames along outer edges of leaded panel, with horseshoe nails and lead scraps.

> **Helpful hint** Hammer the horseshoe nails into the project board only enough to secure them firmly. Most of the nail must protrude above the board so it can be easily removed by hand and used on another section of the panel. Use 10 to 20 nails, depending on the size of the project. Each nail can be used many times and on innumerable projects.

Soldering the panel

Once leading is complete, each juncture where 2 or more cames intersect must be soldered to create a sturdy framework for the stained glass panel. Use a chisel-tipped, 100-watt soldering iron with a built-in temperature control or an iron regulated by a rheostat. Always solder in a well ventilated area and on a level work surface. See **Safety practices and equipment** (p13) before soldering.

Preparing to solder

1 Plug in the soldering iron. Moisten a natural fiber sponge with water and place in the holder on the soldering iron stand.
2 Abrade each came joint with a small wire brush to clean and remove oxidation from the came surfaces.
3 Fill any gaps with a small scrap of H-channel lead came.
4 Pour a small amount of flux into a separate container and replace the cap on the flux bottle. Unwind several inches of 60/40 solder wire from the spool.

Soldering came joints

5 Using a cotton swab or a small brush, dab flux onto the nearest corner joint. Grasp the soldering iron handle like a hammer, in your writing hand, and remove from the stand. With the solder spool in your other hand, hold the end of the unwound solder wire against the fluxed came joint. Apply the flat side of the hot iron tip to the solder and lightly press the tip to the came, melting the solder to the came. Hold the iron tip to the joint a few seconds to melt the solder evenly to the came. Lift the iron tip and the remaining solder wire up and

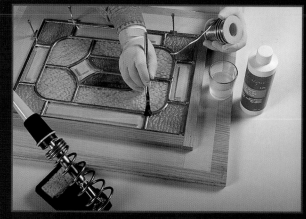

Before soldering, brush each came joint with a wire brush to remove oxidation. Apply flux to joint to aid solder to fuse to came.

With the hot iron tip, melt the solder to the fluxed joint.

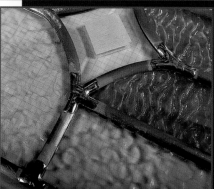

Soldered joints should be smooth and slightly rounded.

...ce along the overlapping came leaf to ...ify that the glass piece fits properly. The ...ced line should run parallel to the edge ...he glass.

away from the came and allow the joint to cool. Soldered joint should be smooth and slightly rounded. Solder the remaining joints in the same manner. At regular intervals, wipe the soldering iron tip on the water-moistened sponge to remove flux residue and prevent the tip from becoming too hot and melting the lead.

6 Flux and solder each remaining came joint on this side of the panel. When soldering joints where several cames meet, melt the solder to the joint and then branch out onto each fluxed came leaf, approximately $\frac{1}{4}$ in. Keep the iron tip in full contact with the came leaf as the solder is pulled from the center of the joint and extended farther out onto each came leaf. If required, apply more solder to achieve a smoothly soldered joint.

7 Cool. Wipe off excess flux with a damp cloth and neutralizing solution.

8 Remove horseshoe nails. Turn panel over (p59) and solder joints on opposite side.

Helpful hints for leading a stained glass panel

- Widen came channel using a lathekin to fit thick glasses, or bevel glass edges by holding at a 45° angle to the grinder and beveling both sides of glass.
- Use the lathekin to ease glass pieces into the came channel and tap outer edge of glass with glazing hammer.
- Lead circular pieces before fitting them in with surrounding pieces. When a pattern requires the use of a number of glass jewels or bevels of the same size, tightly wrap a piece of stretched lead came several times around a cylindrical object that is similar in size to the pieces being leaded. Wood doweling and empty solder spools are ideal. Slip the spiral off the cylinder and insert a jewel into the end coil. Mark and trim the coil so that it completely encases the circumference of the jewel. Repeat for each required piece. When fitting the jewel into the panel, align the juncture where the 2 ends of the came circle meet with an adjacent intersecting came joint.
- To aid in fitting or to verify that a piece of glass is accurately seated in the came channel, use a marker to trace along the overlapping came leaf and onto the glass. Remove the glass piece from the came and observe how closely the edge of the glass relates to the traced line. The edges of a properly fitted glass piece will run parallel to the traced line, with an even margin showing along the edges that allows for the depth of the channel. Grind or groze away portions of the glass edge that do not duplicate the traced line.
- If glass pieces are loose in channels, they may be too small. Hold in place with shims—slivers of lead came positioned against the heart in one of the came channels. If a gap is still present, the piece is still too small and must be re-cut.
- When horseshoe nails are not appropriate, use masking tape to hold glass pieces in place. (See photo.)

Helpful hints for soldering a leaded glass panel

- Do not hold soldering iron tip to lead came longer than necessary or lead can melt away. If this happens allow the lead to cool, cut a small piece of lead to place over the hole in the came, apply flux, and solder the joint as normal.
- Zinc and other rigid cames require more heat for a proper solder joint. Apply flux and heat to the came for a few seconds with the flat side of the iron tip. Once heated, the solder will fuse to the zinc came properly.
- When soldering joints where zinc and lead cames meet, always heat and apply solder to the zinc came first.
- Use a wooden craft stick or a piece of wood doweling to hold lead came in place while soldering.
- If solder will not melt and flow smoothly, clean the came joint with a small wire brush to remove oxidation and apply flux so that the solder will flow and bond smoothly to the came. Be sure iron tip is at the proper temperature for the type of came being soldered, and wipe the hot iron tip on the water-moistened sponge frequently to remove flux residue and to cool the tip.
- Check the panel to verify that all came joints have been soldered (one may be overlooked).

Turning over large panels

A Position longest side of wood project board flush with the edge of work surface. Remove any wood trim pieces along this side. Pull the panel towards you until it is suspended halfway over the edge of the work surface. Grasp the edge of the panel farthest from you with one hand and use your other hand to cup the edge closest to you. Tilt the panel forward into a vertical position. Use the edge of the work surface for support and leverage as you raise panel upright and its weight is transferred to your cupped hand. Lower the panel onto the work surface in one of 2 different ways:

• Keeping the panel vertical, rotate so that front side is facing away from you. Position so that middle of panel is flush against the edge of the work surface again, and tilt and slide panel onto the work surface. OR

• Once vertical, rest the bottom edge of the panel on the work surface. Tilt the top edge towards you (while supporting the front of the panel) until the panel is lying flat on the work surface.

B Ask a friend for assistance and use wood project board for support. With wood trim pieces still secured to the project board and helping to hold the panel in place, slide the board over the edge of the work surface and into a vertical position. Resting the bottom edge of the project board on the floor, remove the panel while keeping it vertical at all times. Grasping the panel by its side edges, turn the panel around and place it back on the project board. Lift and slide the project board back onto the work surface.

Cementing and cleaning the panel

1 Lay panel on work surface covered with newspaper. Wipe off flux with a damp cloth and neutralizing solution. Dry with soft cloth.

2 Stir cement compound thoroughly. Consistency should be like mud. If too stiff, add turpentine; if too thin, add whiting.

3 Scoop some cement onto the surface of the panel. With a soft-bristled brush, gently force the cement under each came leaf and into the channels, using a circular motion.

4 With the flat end of the lathekin, carefully press the leaf of wider, flat-profiled lead cames closed and against the glass surface, trapping the cement within the channels.

5 Remove excess cement from the glass with the brush or your gloved hand and put back into container.

6 Sprinkle whiting over the cemented side of panel. Allow a few minutes for whiting to absorb some of the moisture from the cement.

7 Run a toothpick or wood skewer along the leaf edge of each came to remove excess cement and whiting.

8 Brush the panel along the length of the cames (rubbing across may loosen cement within the channels). Whisk residual cement and whiting off panel and discard.

9 Spread whiting on the panel to

> **NOTE** Always wear a dust mask or respirator (equipped with filters designed to screen out dust and abrasives) when working with whiting.

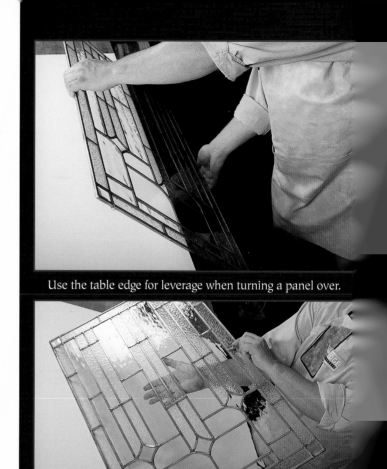

Use the table edge for leverage when turning a panel over.

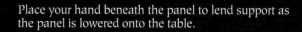

Place your hand beneath the panel to lend support as the panel is lowered onto the table.

Force cement under the cames with a soft-bristled brush.

Use flat end of lathekin to press came leaf closed, trapping cement within the channel.

Run a pointed wooden stick along leaf edge to separate cement in channel from excess cement and whiting on panel surface.

Rub brush lenthwise along cames when removing excess cement and whiting from glass surface.

Helpful hints
- Cement can be difficult to remove from textured glasses or sandblasted areas. Before cementing, cover these glass surfaces with masking tape. Do not tape past the visible glass surface onto the leaf of the cames.
- Use a shop vacuum to remove excess whiting and cement from the panel's surface.

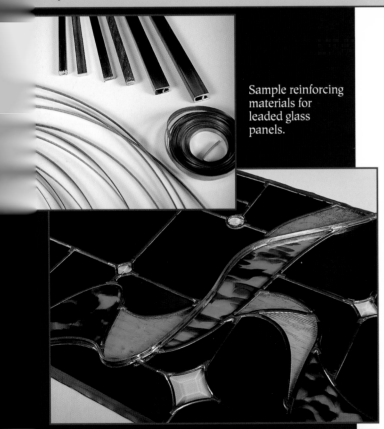

Sample reinforcing materials for leaded glass panels.

NOTE To minimize the damaging effects of moisture, extreme climates, and changing temperatures, leaded panels should be installed towards the interior of the building with a sealed glass unit or a protective sheet of float glass between the panel, and the outdoors.

absorb any remaining oils, flux, dirt, or cement and polish until clean with a clean brush. Use a toothbrush or wood stick to remove cement collected in corners or along came edges.

10 Turn panel and cement opposite side, following above steps.

11 Panel should lie flat until cement has dried (24 to 48 hours). When required, leaded glass panels can be cleaned with an ammonia-free commercial window cleaner and a soft cloth.

Reinforcing leaded glass panels
Reinforcement to prevent sagging and warping may be required for panels
- larger than 4 square feet,
- made up of many small pieces,
- having uninterrupted straight lines, or
- exposed to the elements.

For support that is undetectable as part of the panel's internal framework, use one of the following:

Re-strip   thin strips of copper or brass, strong yet flexible, inserted into the channel of lead cames. Or use copper-coated steel strip for greater internal support.

Reinforced and metal-covered lead came   a heart augmented with a brass strip or a steel wire is the most flexible.

Zinc, brass, and copper cames   eliminate the need for additional reinforcement. Ideal for use in geometric and linear patterns. Zinc U-channel came is often recommended as the border came for free-hanging leaded panels because of its rigidity.

Larger panels may require supplementary reinforcement bars fastened to the back of a completed leaded glass panel. They will protrude slightly from the panel surface. To make the final cleaning easier and to prevent glass breakage, cement and clean both sides of the panel before attaching the bars.

Steel bars   that are positioned horizontally, 20 in to 24 in apart, across the back of the panel, to extend to the outside edges of the opposing border cames, must be secured with heavy-gauge copper wires soldered to the panel interior and border cames. Because they are not easily bent, the bars may be visible through the glass unless they have been placed along a horizontal pattern line.

Zinc and zinc-coated steel rebar   are positioned on the back of the panel in the same manner as steel bars. Zinc rebar is a popular choice because it is lighter, not as thick as steel, and can be bent at an angle or follow slight curves to align with the interior pattern lines, making it less noticeable. It can be soldered directly onto interior and border cames.

> **Cement recipe** Mix together 2 cups plaster of Paris, 1 cup Portland cement, and 4 cups whiting (calcium carbonate); add and stir until smooth 1 cup double boiled linseed oil, and $1\frac{1}{2}$ cups turpentine. Follow all safety precautions listed on manufacturer's packaging.

Replacing broken glass pieces in leaded panels

For panels assembled using lead cames with a flat profile

1 Cover the work surface with several layers of newspaper. Place the panel face down so broken glass piece can be removed and replaced from the back side of the panel.

2 Use lead cutters to cut through each solder joint where the cames butt against each other around broken glass piece.

3 Run the blade of a lead knife several times between the glass piece and the leaf of the surrounding cames to separate cement from glass surface.

4 Use the flat end of a lathekin to pry back the leaf of the surrounding cames until they are at right angles to the glass surface. Use lead cutters to snip away the soldered ends of the cames if they are too rigid to bend back.

5 For easier removal, the glass may have to be broken into smaller pieces. Score with a glass cutter. On the underside of the glass, tap along the score lines with the end of the cutter, being careful not to crack the glass pieces next to it. When the score lines "run" and break into smaller pieces, remove the fragments with pliers.

6 Scrape away all cement and glass fragments from came channels with knife blade.

7 Use panel's pattern as a guide to cut a new glass piece. Grind or groze to fit.

8 Use the lathekin to press the leaf of the cames into their original position and onto the surface of the replacement glass piece.

9 Trim pieces of lead scraps to fill any gaps in the came joints. Flux and solder all came joints around the piece.

10 Clean and cement the area around the replaced glass piece.

For panels assembled using lead cames with rounded profile or flat cames difficult to pry back

1 Follow steps 1 to 3, as outlined above.

2 Use a utility knife to cut away the leaf on each lead came that overlaps onto the broken glass piece. Lead cames with a rounded profile are almost impossible to pry back.

3 Follow steps 5 to 7, outlined above, to remove broken glass piece and cut replacement.

4 Wrap and burnish the edges of the replacement piece with copper foil (see **Applying copper foil** on p80). Place the foiled piece within the opening. Use a utility knife to trim the copper foil to align with the adjacent lead cames.

5 Flux and solder the foiled piece to the surrounding lead cames. Try to achieve an even solder seam like the came profile. Let the area cool occasionally to prevent melting of the lead came. See **Bead soldering** (p81).

6 Clean the soldered area with warm water and neutralizing solution. Dull the brighter finish of the solder seams by rubbing them with cement and whiting.

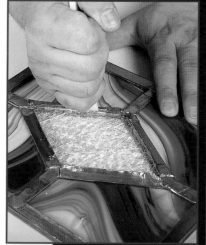
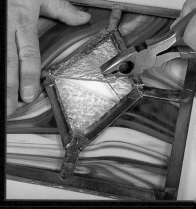

A lathekin is used to bend back leaf of flat profile cames.

Remove broken glass pieces with pliers.

With flat end of lathekin, press the came leaf to glass surface.

6

Use a utility knife to cut away overlapping leaf of round profile came.

Solder along foiled edge and remaining portion of leaf to create an even, rounded solder seam.

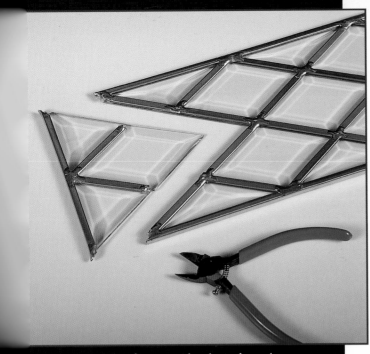

eparate came joints from outside edges of panel to cames round broken piece, insert new piece and reassemble.

For panels assembled using rigid cames (zinc, brass, or copper)

1 The leaf of these cames cannot be pried back or cut away. The came joints, from the outside edges of the panel to the cames around the broken glass, will have to be separated. Survey the panel carefully and map out a strategy that will require severing the fewest came joints. Draw a line with a marker at each point where a joint is to be cut.

2 Use a pattern copy or trace the outline of the panel onto a sheet of paper. The outline will serve as a guide when the sections of the panel are to be reassembled.

3 Cut through the solder on the marked joints with lead cutters. Turn the panel over and cut the opposing joints on the other side of the panel.

4 Pull away detached section(s) and remove the broken piece of glass.

5 Cut a new piece of glass, using the pattern copy or a template as your guide.

6 Insert the new piece into the cames and reassemble the sections of the panel on the pattern outline. Once assembled, fasten horseshoe nails along the panel's perimeter to hold the sections of the panel together.

7 Flux and solder all came joints that had been detached.

8 Clean and cement as required.

Helpful hints
• When a pattern copy is not available, make a template of the broken glass piece.
—If all the fragments of the broken piece are present, assemble and tape the fragments together to form a template.
—Position a piece of clear float glass over the broken piece and draw the outline of the glass shape with a marker, tracing along the middle of the leaf of each surrounding came. With a glass cutter, cut the traced shape inside the marker line. Remove broken piece from panel, place template in opening, and grind or groze for accurate template.
• When cutting through a solder joint is not possible, cut a strip of aluminum from an empty soda can with utility scissors. To safely grip the strip, wrap one end with masking tape.
—Apply a hot iron tip to the came joint, taking care not to melt the underlying came. As the solder on the joint becomes molten, draw the iron tip across the joint, pulling solder away with the iron tip. Wipe the excess solder off the tip and onto the water-moistened sponge.
—Heat the joint with the hot iron tip, and separate the cames butted together by wedging the aluminum strip between them.

Assemble and tape fragments of broken pieces together to form a template. Trace outline onto a new piece of glass.

Leaded Glass Projects & Patterns

Twilight
BEGINNER PANEL

Dimensions   10 in wide by 14 in high
No. of pieces   16
Glass required   Letters identify type of glass used on pattern (p66).
- **A**   6 in x 11 in pink and white wispy ripple
- **B**   7 in x 11 in iridescent clear hammer
- **C**   1—3 in clear star bevel
- **D**   1—2 in clear star bevel
- **E**   2—1½ in x 4 in clear rectangular bevels
- **F**   2—1½ in x 8 in clear rectangular bevels

This quantity of glass is the exact amount needed for the pattern. You may wish to purchase more glass to allow for matching textures and grain.

Additional Materials & Tools Required

Materials	Tools
1 length of ¼ in U-channel zinc came	small square
2 lengths of ¼ in H-channel lead came	needlenose pliers
14-gauge tinned copper wire	
2 cup hook screws	
linked metal chain	

NOTE Quantities of cames listed are based on a 6 ft length.

Instructions

Assemble this elegant panel using **How-to techniques** (p53–60).

1 Refer to **Preparing the pattern** (p53) and make 2 full-size copies of pattern (p66). Use one copy to cut glass pieces to correct shape and size. Use second copy for leading the panel. If opalescent glass is used, make a third copy and cut out the necessary pattern pieces for use as tracing templates (p15).

2 Use the marker to trace (p14) each pattern piece on the glass to be cut.

3 Cut (pp15–19) **inside** the marker line for each piece of glass required. This will give greater accuracy and fit of pieces. Use the cork-backed straightedge to score straight lines (p18).

4 Set up project board (p54). Fasten wood trim along one side and one end of the pattern, forming a right angle in the corner where you will start the leading process.

5 Cut (p55) 4 pieces of zinc U-channel came to form the border. Trim both ends of each border came to an inward 45° angle.

6 Put border cames in position and assemble the panel (see **Leading the panel**, p56).

7 Solder (p57) each corner and came joint on the front side of the panel.

8 Turn (p59) the panel over and solder each corner and came joint on opposite side.

9 For each hanging loop required for a small leaded panel, cut a 1 in piece of tinned wire and bend it over a pencil to form a U shape.

10 Gripping the middle of the loop in the jaws of the needlenose pliers, position the ends of the loop over the zinc border came and onto the came joint on either side of the panel (marked on pattern). Apply a dab of flux and solder securely in place. Turn the panel over and repeat on the opposite side. The loop should be firmly attached to the zinc and lead cames on both sides of the panel.

11 Cement and clean the panel (p59).

12 Screw the cup hooks into the window frame and hang the panel using a linked metal chain strong enough to bear the panel weight.

For additional support, solder hanging loop to zinc border came as well as to adjacent lead came.

Helpful hints
- Place masking tape on the underside and over the raised surface of the bevels for protection from scratches.
- If bevels or bevel clusters are not available, substitute with complementary art glass.

64

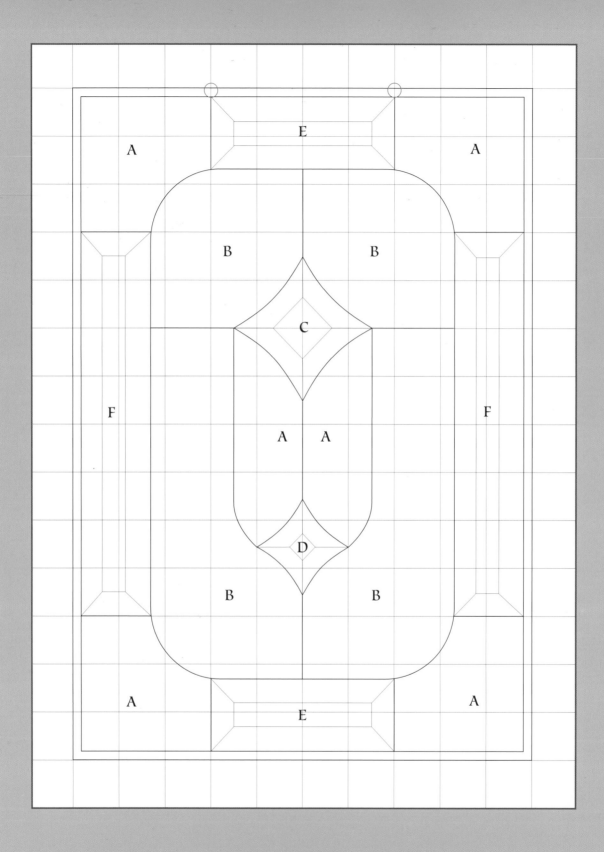

Touch of Frost

WINDOW PANEL

Dimensions   34 in wide by 22 in high
No. of pieces   53
Glass required   Letters identify type of glass used on pattern (p68).

    A   9 in x 12 in dark amber semi-antique
    B   16 in x 15 in green, cerise ruby, and clear granite
    C   18 in x 12 in translucent white glue chip
    D   18 in x 30 in clear 4mm architectural (Autumn pattern)
    E   12 in x 18 in yellow and white opal with brown streamers and
yellow, orange, and brown fractures
    F   15 in x 12 in clear with green streamers and orange, red, and
yellow fractures
    G   4—35mm circular white opal double-faceted jewels
    H   8—2 in x 2 in clear square bevels
    I   1—3 in x 3 in clear square glue chip bevel

Additional Materials & Tools Required

Materials	Tools
2 lengths of ½ in U-channel zinc came	small square
5 lengths of ¼ in H-channel lead came	
1 length of 5⁄16 in H-channel lead came	
wood frame	
2 heavy-duty cup hooks	
2 heavy-duty screw hooks	
linked metal chain	

NOTE   Quantities of cames listed are based on a 6 ft length.

This quantity of glass is the exact amount needed for the pattern. You may wish to purchase more glass to allow for matching textures and grain.

Instructions

The transition from autumn to winter is the main influence behind the glass selection for this classically styled window panel. Refer to **How-to techniques** (pp53–60) for specific instructions on leading a stained glass panel.

1 Follow steps 1 to 8 as described for **Twilight Beginner Panel** (p64). Note **Helpful hint** regarding bevels.

2 Cement and clean the panel (p59).

3 This leaded glass panel is installed into an oak frame made to fit this panel. You can make your frame or hire a professional. Frame opening should be 34⅛ in x 22⅛ in, allowing for discrepancies in the panel's size. Fasten a heavy-duty screw hook into frame's top 2 corners 1 in from the frame's outside edge. Screw the cup hooks into window frame and hang the panel using

NOTE a) You can lead the pattern lines around the thicker pieces of clear 4mm architectural glass (D) with an H-channel lead came that has a high heart.
b) Use the wider 5⁄16 in H-channel came to lead the outside perimeter of the glass pieces (E), to accent the central circular design motif.

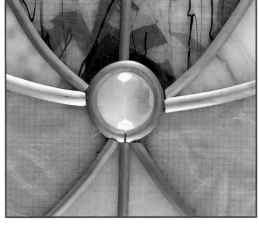

Varying came widths add visual interest. See *Helpful hints*, p58, for instruction on leading circular jewels.

a linked metal chain strong enough to bear the panel weight.

Option   Do not frame but attach hanging loops to zinc border cames.

1 Cut a 2 in piece of heavy-gauge tinned wire for each hanging loop and bend it over a pencil to form a U shape.

2 Attach a hanging loop at 2 side border cames. Gripping the middle of the loop with needlenose pliers, position the ends of the loop over the top edge of the zinc border came and onto the leaf of the came on either side of the panel. Apply flux to the tinned wire and the border came on the top side and solder securely in place. Turn the panel over and repeat on the opposite side. The loop should now be firmly attached to the zinc came on both sides of the panel.

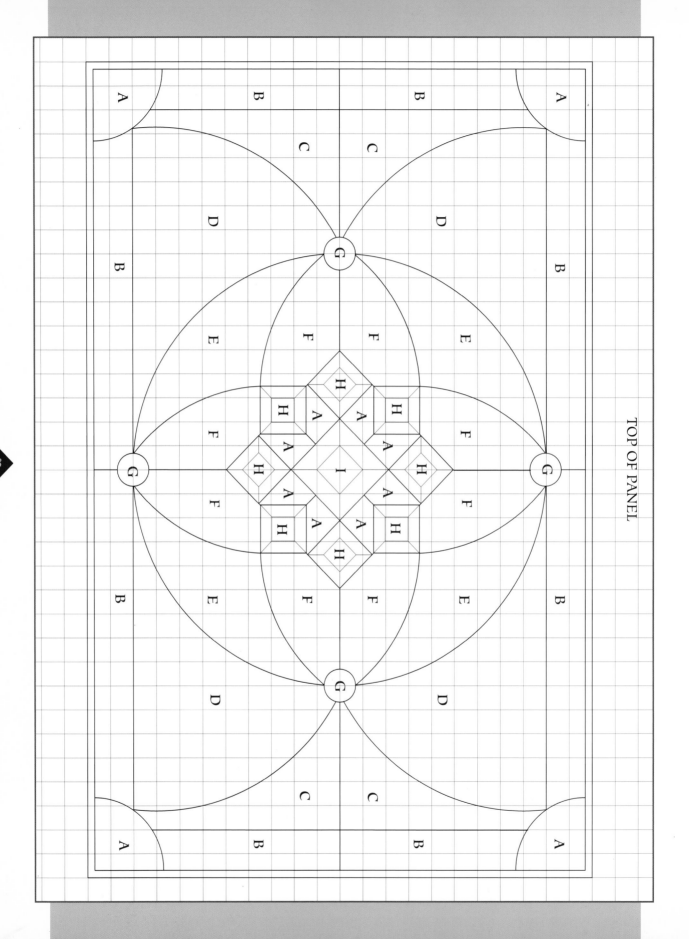

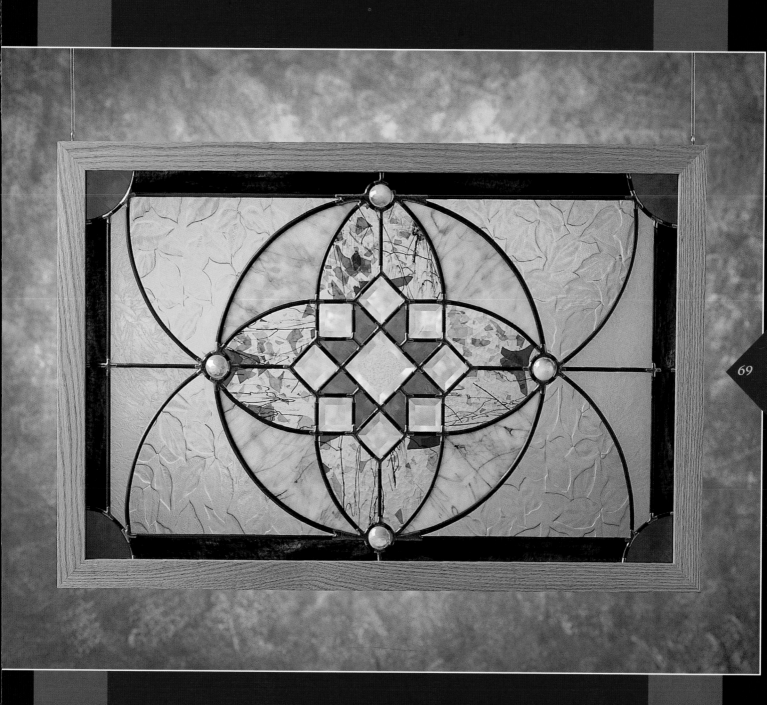

Peaks

WINDOW PANEL

Dimensions   21 in diameter
No. of pieces   21
Glass required   Letters identify type of glass used on pattern (p72).

- **A**   21 in x 8 in violet semi-antique
- **B**   24 in x 5 in translucent white glue chip
- **C**   20 in x 12 in cobalt blue and emerald green ring mottle
- **D**   10 in x 10 in clear 4mm architectural (Croco pattern)
- **E**   7 in x 4 in clear ripple
- **F**   2—2 in x 4 in clear diamond bevels
- **G**   1—2 in x 3 in clear diamond bevel
- **H**   1—4 in clear circular bevel

Additional Materials & Tools Required

Materials	Tools
1 length of ¼ in U-channel zinc came	compass
3 lengths of ³⁄₁₆ in H-channel lead came	sidecutters
14-gauge tinned copper wire	needlenose pliers
2 cup hook screws	
linked metal chain	

NOTE   Quantities of cames listed are based on a 6 ft length.

This quantity of glass is the exact amount needed for the pattern. You may wish to purchase more glass to allow for matching textures and grain.

Instructions

The circular outline of this abstract panel complements the angular peaks and curving lines of mountain mist.

Getting started

1   Follow steps 1 to 3 in **Twilight Beginner Panel** (p64). Note **Helpful hint** regarding bevels.

2   Tape a copy of the pattern onto a project board 24 in x 24 in.

3   Use a compass to draw a **sight** line on the pattern that has a diameter of 20½ in. A sight line is determined by the width of the border came (in this case ¼ in), and defines the area of glass that is visible once the border came is in place.

4   Hammer horseshoe nails 3 in apart along pattern sight line into wood project board, with the flat side of each nail parallel to the sight line.

Forming the zinc border came

The circular form of the panel requires that the came be bent into shape before assembling. It can be bent manually or by a metal came bender, that bends the came to the desired size of circle without kinking the metal. Most stained glass studios have a came bender or you can purchase one.

Bending zinc border came manually

5   Place the middle of the came length against the outer edges of the horseshoe nails along the sight line at the bottom of the pattern. The came's channel must be facing towards the center of the panel.

6   Begin shaping the came by securing horseshoe nails along the outside edge of the came. Starting in the middle of the came length, work your way around the panel outline on either side. To hold the came in place and retain the shape, hammer in nails opposite to the ones along the sight line.

7   Trim the ends of the came until they butt against each other to complete the border.

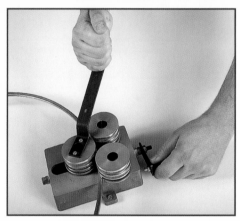

Rigid cames can easily be bent when turned through the wheels of a metal came bender.

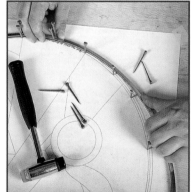

Draw a sight line on the pattern to act as a guide when manually bending border came.

Start at the bottom when assembling a round leaded panel.

70

The ends should be aligned with one of the pattern lines that intersect with the border at the top of the panel. The zinc came border is now formed to the correct size and held firmly in place by horseshoe nails fastened on either side of the came.

Assembling the panel

8 Starting at the bottom, assemble the panel following **Leading the panel** (p56). As the last few glass pieces are leaded near the top of the panel, remove several of the horseshoe nails securing the ends of the border came. Pull back the border came only enough to insert and lead the remaining glass pieces. Once completed, press the border came back into its correct position and anchor in place with horseshoe nails. (See photograph, **Turning Point 3-Panel Screen**, p73.)

9 Follow steps 7 to 12 for the **Twilight Beginner Panel** (p64) to complete and hang the panel.

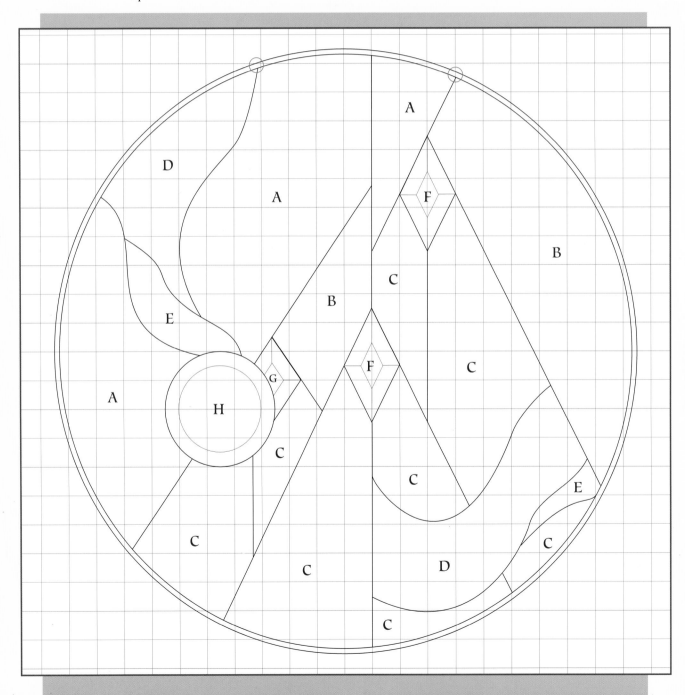

Turning Point

3-Panel Screen

Dimensions	16 in wide by 61 in high (each panel)	
No. of pieces	125	
Glass required	Letters identify type of glass used on pattern (p74).	
A	11 sq ft clear 4mm architectural (sandblasted Delta pattern)	
B	5 sq ft clear 4mm architectural (Croco pattern)	
C	1 sq ft red hand-rolled cathedral	
D	1 sq ft clear semi-antique	
E	2 sq ft clear with black streamers and black frit	
F	1 sq ft clear with black streamers and white fractures	
G	4 sq ft clear with black swirl	
H	4 sq ft clear with white swirl	
J	1½ sq ft black fibroid	

Additional Materials & Tools Required

Materials	Tools
8 lengths of ½ in U-channel zinc came	small square
8 lengths of ¼ in H-channel zinc came	miter came saw,
6 lengths of ⅜ in H-channel zinc came	sidecutters or hacksaw
4 lengths of ½ in H-channel zinc came	small metal file
wood frame for a 3-panel screen	

NOTE Quantities of cames listed are based on a 6 ft length.

This quantity of glass is the exact amount needed for the pattern. You may wish to purchase more glass to allow for matching textures and grain. Due to the larger size of this project, glass quantities have been listed in square footage

Instructions

The panels for this striking, contemporary screen are built using basic lead came construction techniques. Zinc came is chosen for rigidity and strength. However, lead came can be used with the addition of reinforcement bars.

1 To assemble each of the panels, follow steps 1 to 5 for **Twilight Panel** (p64). We used ½ in U-channel zinc came. H-channel came can be substituted when the border came may have to be trimmed to fit the opening. For added visual effect, we cut clear architectural glass (B) with the textured side face up for some pieces and face down for others.

2 Secure the appropriate border cames in position and proceed to assemble the panel as described in **Leading the panel** (p56). Refer to **Cutting zinc and other rigid metal cames** (p55) for additional instruction. Use ¼ in came for all straight horizontal lines; ⅜ in came for all straight vertical lines; ½ in came for the large curving outer arcs; and a combination of ¼ in and ⅜ in came for areas inside these large arcs.

3 Solder (p57) each corner and came joint on the front side of the panel. Align extending came leafs along their corresponding pattern lines and solder securely to the came joints.

4 Turn (p59) panel over and solder each corner and came joint as well as any came leaf extensions on the opposite side.

5 Cement and clean the panel (p59).

6 Once completed the panels can be installed into the wood frame. When constructing a wood frame, make the openings ⅛ in wider and ⅛ in higher than the panel dimensions to allow for discrepancies.

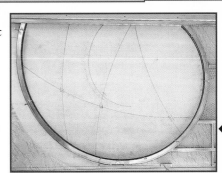

Pre-form came for large curves. Draw a sight line to act as a guide.

Remove heart from portions of zinc cames that extend onto glass surface.

NOTE On each panel pattern, several pattern lines extend over onto the adjacent glass piece. To achieve this effect use one of 2 methods. For shorter lines, cut the H-channel came to the extended length. Use lead cutters to remove the heart from the portion of came leaf that overlaps onto the adjacent glass piece. For longer lines, cut came to fit between the adjacent cames and lead pattern line as normal. Cut a piece of came to correspond with the extension of the pattern line and remove the heart.

Leaf extensions will fit over the glass surface on both sides.

Pull came back to fit last few glass pieces into curved area.

The 2 remaining came leafs can be soldered into position, on either side of the panel, when the came joints are soldered together. Regardless of the method used, cut the ends of the came at a blunt angle and remove any burrs along the cut edge with a small metal file.

The middle panel has a large curving design line in the lower portion that ideally should be leaded with one piece of came. To make leading easier, cut and preform the zinc came to the correct size and shape before assembling the panel. If possible, use a metal came bender to shape the came. To form it manually, see **Bending zinc border came manually**, p70. Lead the remainder of the panel.

Curved came is put back after last pieces have been leaded.

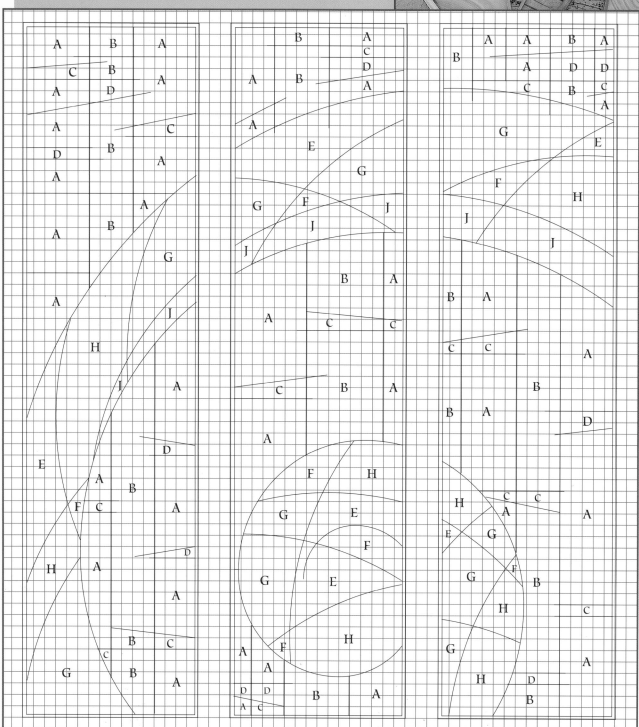

Northern Lights

DOOR AND SIDELIGHT INSERTS

Door panel	Sidelight
Dimensions 20 in wide by 64 in high	7 in wide by 64 in high
No. of pieces 85	49

Glass required   Letters identify type of glass used on pattern (p78).

- **A** 5½ sq ft steel blue full-antique
- **B** 24 in x 12 in steel blue cathedral
- **C** 12 in x 12 in iridescent clear texture
- **D** 8 in x 12 in green craquel
- **E** 16 in x 20 in green and blue streaky full-antique
- **F** 6 in x 7 in ice white, silver yellow, and purple opalescent
- **G** 5 sq ft violet, white, and clear streaky full-antique
- **H** 10 in x 8 in dark purple full-antique
- **I** 16 in x 14 in medium purple semi-antique
- **J** 15 in x 9 in light purple full-antique
- **K** 24 in x 16 in green, blue, and purple streaky
- **L** 3—1 in clear square bevels
- **M** 1—1½ in clear star bevel
- **N** 1—3 in clear star bevel
- **P** 1—2 in x 3 in clear diamond bevel
- **Q** 1—24mm clear circular faceted jewel
- **R** 1—30mm clear circular faceted jewel

Additional Materials & Tools Required

Materials	Tools
5 lengths of ½ in H-channel lead came	small square
1 length of 3/16 in H-channel lead came	wide-jawed pliers
11 lengths of ¼ in H-channel lead came	hacksaw or bolt cutters
3 lengths of 3/8 in H-channel lead came	
2 lengths of 1/8 in x 5/16 in zinc rebar	

NOTE Quantities of cames and rebar listed are based on a 6 ft length.

> This quantity of glass is the exact amount needed for the pattern. You may wish to purchase more glass to allow for matching textures and grain.

76

Instructions

Northern lights (aurora borealis) dancing over Lake Winnipeg, the world's eleventh largest freshwater lake, inspired this home entranceway.

1 Follow steps 1 to 4 for **Twilight Beginner Panel** (p64). See **Helpful hint** regarding bevels (p64).

2 Cut (p55) 4 pieces of ½ in H-channel lead came for border of each panel. See **Border cames—architectural panels** (p55). NOTE The ends of each border came should be cut at a right angle and butted flush against one another, not mitered at a 45° angle as in previous projects. Cut the side pieces to fit the full length of the panel but cut end pieces 1 in shorter to accommodate the ½ in width of each side came. The door panel requires 2—64 in side pieces and 2—19 in end pieces. The sidelight requires 2—64 in side pieces and 2—6 in end pieces.

3 Follow steps 6 to 8 for **Twilight Beginner Panel** (p64).

4 Cement and clean the panels (p59).

Reinforcing the panels

Review **Reinforcing leaded glass panels** (p60). These panels need additional support for strength and to prevent stretching and sagging over time. We have used zinc rebar because it can be bent to conform to pattern lines, making it less obvious to the eye than heavier steel reinforcing bars.

Use pliers to bend rebar to conform to pattern line and horseshoe nails to hold rebar in place.

Solder rebar to each came joint and to several points along came length.

5 Use a pattern copy, taped to the project board (or the work surface), as a guide for bending the rebar to the shape of the highlighted design lines. With one end overlapping the pattern **perimeter line** (p53) by 6 in, secure that end of the rebar to the project board with several horseshoe nails hammered in securely on either side. Place rebar so that its width is perpendicular to the pattern copy and its thinnest edge is centered on the designated **pattern line** (p53) at the point where it intersects with the **cutting line** (p53).

6 Use wide-jawed pliers to bend and manipulate the rebar to the pattern lines using horseshoe nails to hold rebar in position, centered on pattern line.

7 Mark rebar at points ⅛ in from the inside edge of the perimeter line on either side of the panel. Remove the horseshoe nails and the rebar from the project board and cut away excess rebar with a hacksaw or bolt cutters. Continue by shaping each rebar required for the panels.

8 Once each piece of rebar has been shaped to follow the lead lines, attach rebars to back side of panels. Starting at one end, flux and solder the rebar to each came joint and the border cames. Solder on either side of the rebar and at several points along longer lengths of lead came.

78 ▶ **9** Wash away flux residue with a neutralizing solution and warm water. Dull the brighter finish of the solder seams by rubbing them with cement and whiting.

Installing the inserts

These panels are installed onto a standard exterior steel door unit that contains triple-pane sealed units suited to extreme temperature changes. The leaded glass panels are slightly larger than the sealed glass units and are secured to the door and sidelight using wood moldings creating air space between them and the sealed units. We used brass screws to fasten the moldings to the wood trim pieces. The rebars are facing inwards, towards the sealed units. Because the rebars protrude from the surface of the panels, we trimmed the ends that overlap onto the side border cames at an angle, so the panels fit between the molding and the wood trim around the sealed units. Trimming the ends should be done before soldering the rebar to the panel. (See photo.)

Other door units may not suit this method of installation. Consult with an experienced carpenter if you do not have the necessary experience to complete an installation. Interior french-style doors do not require sealed units so the panels can be installed directly into the openings and secured with wood moldings on either side of the panel.

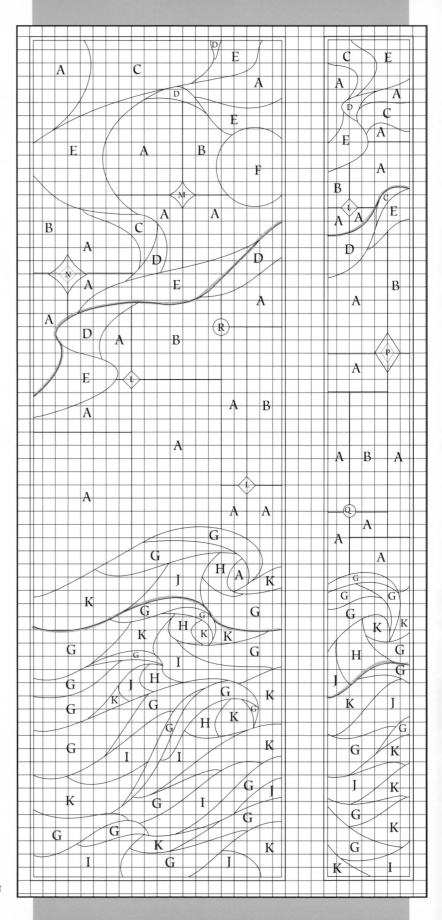

ORANGE HIGHLIGHTED LINES ON PATTERN DENOTE PLACEMENT OF REBAR.

Copper foil construction

Stained glass projects constructed with the copper foil technique are assembled in the following sequence:

1 Draw pattern to correct scale and make 2 or 3 accurate copies.

2 Cut and grind glass pieces to fit pattern.

3 Wrap glass pieces with copper foil.

4 Arrange glass pieces on pattern, creating a copper foil seam between the pieces.

5 Apply molten solder to seam, forming a supportive structure that joins glass pieces together and holds them in place.

6 Apply patina, clean with neutralizing solution, and polish with protective wax compound.

Materials	Tools
2 copies of pattern	apron
newspaper	safety glasses
wood board and trim	utility knife or scissors
masking tape	permanent fine-tipped marker
glass for project	lathekin or fid
cutter oil	cork-backed straightedge
copper foil	glass cutter
safety flux	running pliers
60/40 solder	breaking/combination pliers
neutralizing solution	hammer and nails
patina	glass grinder
wax or finishing compound	soft cloths
	soldering iron and stand
	natural fiber sponge
	cotton swabs
	rubber or latex gloves
	fine steel wool (000)
	toothbrush

Additional listings are given for projects with specific requirements.

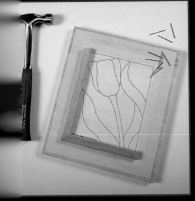

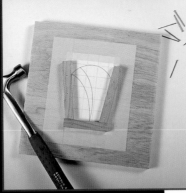

For panels, attach wood trim along one side and one end of pattern.

For 3-dimensional projects, attach wood trim on both sides and narrowest end.

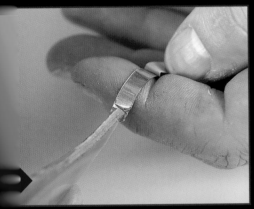

Start foil on a corner of glass piece that will be positioned towards center of panel.

Glass should be centered on foil with equal amounts of foil showing on either side.

Rotate piece as each edge is wrapped until entire piece is foiled.

How-to techniques

Preparing the pattern

See **Basic techniques** (pp14–20) for preparing the pattern and making copies, cutting glass pieces, and grinding glass edges to fit the pieces to the pattern. Check the points that are specific to copper foil construction.

• Use a permanent fine-tipped marker to make pattern lines $\frac{1}{32}$ in width to allow for the application of copper foil.

• Cut each glass piece on the **inside** of the pattern line to accommodate copper foil and decrease amount of grinding required.

Making a jig

Jigs are especially helpful when constructing 3-dimensional projects composed of multiple panels that need to be the same size and shape. Final assembly will be easier if each panel is accurately fitted together and the project will have a more professional look.

1 Tape a copy of the pattern to a wood board 2 in wider (on each side) than the pattern. Do not tape over pattern outline.

2 Align a length of wood trim along one edge of the pattern and nail in place. The trim should just cover the pattern line.

3 Attach wood trim to 2 or more sides of the pattern. When assembling 3-dimensional projects such as lamp shades or vases, trim is usually nailed along the sides and the narrowest end of each panel in the project. Leave widest end open for easy removal from the jig.

Applying copper foil

Copper foil is available in 36 yd rolls in widths $\frac{1}{8}$ in to $\frac{1}{2}$ in (most commonly used are $\frac{3}{16}$ in, $\frac{7}{32}$ in, and $\frac{1}{4}$ in). Copper foil can also be obtained in 12 in x 12 in sheets to use for overlay techniques. Most projects in this book require $\frac{7}{32}$ in copper foil. When a piece of glass varies in thickness along the edge to be foiled, use a wider copper foil and trim it evenly with a utility knife.

1 Rinse glass pieces under clean running water and dry thoroughly.

2 Choose the backing and width of foil best suited for the project. When glass is translucent and the underside of the copper foil will be visible, use a copper foil with the appropriate color of adhesive. Use regular foil (copper-backed) if seams are to be treated with copper patina, black-backed foil for black seams, and silver-backed foil for seams that are to be left silver. If you are not yet certain what color the seams of your finished project will be, use black-backed copper foil. It will have the appearance of a shadow and is quite unnoticeable regardless of the color of the seams.

3 Peel 2 to 3 in of the paper backing away from the end of the copper foil and grasp the backing lightly between your thumb and index finger. The exposed foil should be draped over the remaining fingers with the adhesive-covered side facing upward.

4 Hold the glass piece in your writing hand, perpendicular to the work surface. Foiling should be started at a corner of the glass piece that will be positioned towards the center of the project. Center the edge of the glass on the foil, leaving an equal amount of foil showing on either side of the piece. Fold the edges of the foil over and press firmly to the glass.

5 Continue wrapping the remaining glass edges. Press the foil onto the piece by sliding the middle and ring fingers of your opposite hand along the bottom edge of the glass. Let the foil slide through the thumb and index finger, automatically peeling the backing away from the foil. You should have a clear view of both sides of the glass as the foil is being applied. Rotate the piece as each edge is wrapped with foil, making sure to keep it centered. Wrap entire piece.

6 Cut the foil with a utility knife or scissors, overlapping the starting edge ¼ in. **Crimp** (fold and press) the edge of the foil onto the surface of the glass, using a lathekin or fid. Take care to crimp foil neatly at the corners of the glass piece so that it is not bulky.

7 **Burnish** (press and rub) the foil firmly to the edges of the glass. This will ensure proper adhesion to the glass when the heated soldering iron is applied to the copper foil during the soldering stage.

8 Trim excess and overlapping foil edges with a utility knife. Do not score the glass surface with the knife blade by applying excess pressure.

Soldering the project

Use a 100-watt soldering iron with built-in temperature control and a chisel-style tip. Always rest the soldering iron in a metal stand, never on the work surface. See **Safety practices and equipment** (p13).

1 Plug in the soldering iron. Moisten a natural fiber sponge with water and place in the holder on the soldering iron stand.

2 Place copper foiled pieces on project pattern. Use a jig for accurate assembling.

3 Pour a small amount of safety flux in a separate container and replace the cap on the flux bottle.

4 Use a cotton swab to dab flux onto the copper foil at a point where at least 2 pieces meet. Unwind several inches of 60/40 solder wire from the spool. Grasp the soldering iron handle like a hammer, in your writing hand, and remove from the stand. Holding the hot iron tip close to the fluxed copper foil, melt a small amount of solder onto the tip. Place the iron tip on the copper foil and hold only long enough for the solder to melt onto the foil, to **tack solder** (join) the pieces together.

5 **Flux** and **tack solder** all the pieces together, making sure to tack wherever 2 or more pieces join. Tack each piece in several spots so it will not move out of position when the entire seam is being soldered. At regular intervals, wipe the tip of the soldering iron on the moistened sponge to remove flux residue. See photograph, p82.

6 **Tinning** Once all the pieces have been tacked together, the exposed copper foil must be coated with a thin, flat layer of solder. First apply flux along the entire length of a foiled seam. Holding the soldering iron in your writing hand, place

Cut foil with utility knife overlapping starting edge.

Crimp and burnish edge onto glass surface.

Trim excess and overlap edges with utility knife.

Helpful hints
• Use popsicle sticks, orange peelers, pens and pencils, and shorter lengths of wood doweling, etc., to **burnish** copper foil to glass.
• Copper foil may tear on a tight inside curve. Instead of crimping the foil over the glass edge try burnishing the foil with the lathekin while pressing it over the edge and onto the glass surface. The friction created while burnishing the foil will cause it to soften slightly, become more pliable, and reduce the risk of tearing.

Frequently wipe iron tip on water-moistened sponge to remove flux residue and cool iron tip.

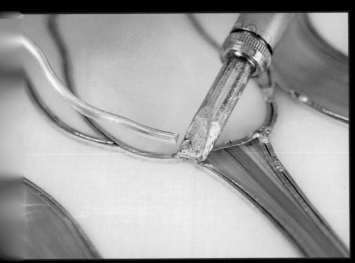

Tack solder pieces together at several locations to prevent pieces from moving out of position while soldering.

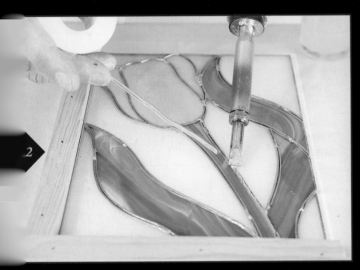

Apply a thin layer of solder (tinning) over all foiled seams before bead soldering.

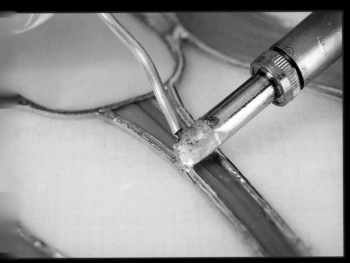

Bead soldering gives seams an even, rounded appearance and provides the support structure for a copper foil project.

the flat side of the iron tip on the fluxed copper foil and grasping the spool of solder in the other hand, place the end of the solder on the tip. As the solder melts, pull the tip along the seam, leaving a thin coating of solder over the foil. This is tinning. Tin each foiled seam and fill in any gaps between the stained glass pieces with solder. See photograph.

7 Bead soldering gives seams a rounded and even finish. Reapply flux along one seam. Place the narrower side of the iron tip onto one end of the seam (the flat side of the tip will now be in a vertical position), keeping the tip in contact with the seam at all times. Holding the solder to the tip, slowly draw the iron along the length of the seam allowing the solder to build up only enough to create a slightly raised, half-round seam. When the solder begins to build up more than necessary, pull the strand of solder away from the iron tip. Draw the tip along the seam until the molten solder levels out more evenly. It will take a bit of practice to determine how quickly to move the iron and how much solder to apply. Because glass can crack if it is heated too much, don't go over a solder seam too many times. If you are not happy with the appearance of a seam, allow the area to cool while you solder another seam. Return to the seam and apply flux and reheat the seam with the iron tip. Only apply more solder if the seam appears to be too flat. Flux and bead solder the remaining seams.

8 Turn the project over after letting the solder seams cool for a few minutes. Tin and bead solder each seam on the reverse side, as described in the steps above.

9 Finish outside edges of a project that will not be utilizing a lead or zinc came border by fluxing and tinning all exposed copper foil on both sides. Holding the project in a vertical position, bead the edge by applying a small amount of solder and then lifting the iron off the foil long enough for it to cool before adding more. Use a touch-and-lift motion rather than drawing the iron along the edge. This will prevent the copper foil from becoming too hot and lifting off the edges of the glass. Proceed around the outside perimeter of the project. Rotate the piece as required to keep the edge being beaded level. If not kept level, gravity will cause the solder to flow away from the area you are beading.

10 Remove all flux residue to eliminate oxidization and tarnishing of the solder seams. (See **Cleaning the project**, p84.)

NOTE If you did not complete soldering and will not be returning to it that day, remove as much of the flux as possible with a damp cloth and a small amount of neutralizing solution.

Common soldering problems and how to avoid them

Solder is not bonding to the copper foil
- Apply flux to the copper foil or molten solder will not bond. Flux may have evaporated. Apply flux and try again.
- Iron tip must be hot and in contact with the foiled and fluxed seam. Both solder and foil must be heated for solder to flow and adhere to foil properly.
- Be sure that the copper foil does not have a layer of oxidization on it. Rub fine steel wool (000) lengthwise along the foil until the seam is shiny again. Apply flux and solder again.

Solder melts through the seams
- Do not hold the soldering tip too long in one place or solder the seam too many times without allowing it to cool. Solder in another area of the project until the seam cools and try again.

Melt-through is occurring due to large gaps between glass pieces
- Cut glass pieces accurately to fit the pattern to prevent gaps which can be responsible for melt-throughs, especially in 3-dimensional projects.

- Tin seams with 50/50 solder, allowing the seams to cool, and then bead solder with 60/40 solder to avoid melt-throughs on 3-dimensional projects. (50/50 solder melts at a higher temperature so melt-throughs will not occur as often if it is used as a base when beading.)
- Place masking tape on the underside of a gap to prevent molten solder from falling through before it cools.

Copper foil is lifting from the glass surface during the soldering stage
- Do not draw the soldering iron tip over a seam too many times without letting the seam cool occasionally. The copper foil is very thin and is an excellent heat conductor; therefore, applying too much heat can cause it to lift away from the glass surface. As well, the adhesive may become soft and runny, losing its grip on the glass edge.
- Check before foiling to ensure that the adhesive backing on the copper foil has not dried out and lost its tackiness.
- Clean glass pieces thoroughly before applying foil to remove all traces of cutter oil and grinding residue.
- Start and end the foil on an edge of the glass piece that will not be on the perimeter of a project (the point where the foil overlaps should be on an inside seam).
- Burnish the foil tightly to the glass by rubbing several times with a lathekin or fid, using a back-and-forth motion.

Solder seams are uneven and have peaks and valleys
- Apply flux and touch up the seam with the soldering iron. Hold the tip on the solder seam long enough to start melting. Lift the tip up and repeat the melt-and-lift motion along the seam, smoothing it out. Add solder, if required.

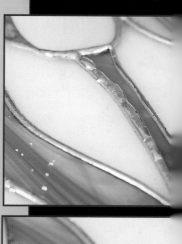

Solder seam has too much solder
- Remove excess solder by melting the solder with the iron and then quickly dragging the iron tip across the seam, pulling excess molten solder with it. Immediately, remove the excess solder from the iron tip by wiping it with a water moistened sponge.

Molten solder and flux are bubbling and spattering while seam is soldered
- Use a safety flux (formulated for stained glass work) sparingly along foiled seams. The application of the hot iron tip and molten solder to a foiled seam can cause excessive amounts of liquid flux to boil and sputter before evaporating. Small solder balls are formed and sprayed about as they contact the bubbling flux and may burn skin. Solder seams may appear rough and unsightly.

Small pits are present in the solder seam
- Soldering over a seam repeatedly can overheat the copper foil adhesive causing it to ooze up from between the foil and the glass. Traces of the adhesive become trapped in the solder, creating small air bubbles in the seam. Let the solder cool slightly and use a cotton swab or paper towel to wipe the adhesive away. Reapply flux and smooth out the solder seam with the iron tip.

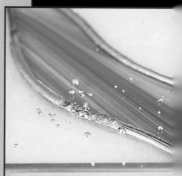

- Use flux sparingly. Too much flux while soldering can also cause a pitted surface on a solder seam.

Solder is not flowing properly, resulting in uneven solder seams
- Apply flux to each foiled seam before attempting to solder. If you have soldered over a seam more than once, the flux may have evaporated. Reapply flux and try again.
- Clean the iron tip regularly on a natural fiber sponge moistened with water, to remove flux residue. If spots are still present on the iron tip, use a tip tinning compound to recoat the tip.
- Adjust temperature controller of soldering iron. The iron tip may not be hot enough to melt the solder or it may be too hot causing the solder to melt through the seams.

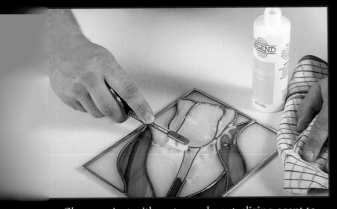

Clean project with water and neutralizing agent to remove flux residue and neutralize patina acids.

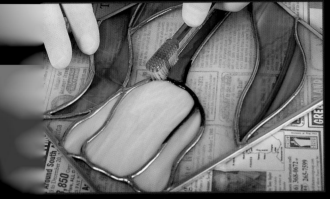

Turn solder seams black or copper by applying appropriate patina.

elpful hints

Some patinas may be applied immediately after soldering thout removing the flux residue. Check the bottle for structions.

The black or copper colored patina is a chemical reaction the surface of the solder seam. It can be removed by bbing with fine steel wool (000).

Copper patina may be affected by minerals in local water, use distilled water to clean and rinse projects. Apply a eral coat of finishing wax and buff the seams vigorously for hiny, copper look.

Stained glass finishing compound or wax will protect and polish solder seams.

Cleaning the project

Clean the project as soon as possible after soldering to remove any flux residue and prevent solder seams from oxidizing and tarnishing.

1 Apply a small amount of neutralizing solution (commercial or sodium bicarbonate mixed with liquid dish detergent) to your project to counteract the corrosive effects of flux.

2 Moisten the neutralizing solution with water and gently scrub the project surface with a soft cloth or an old toothbrush.

3 Rinse under warm, running water to remove flux and cleaner. Do not soak.

4 Dry with a soft, lint-free cloth.

Finishing the project

Solder seams can be left shiny and silver or lightly rubbed with steel wool for a subtler, pewter look. The color of the seams can be altered by applying a black or copper patina. Patina is usually applied after soldering and cleaning. Protect the solder seams from oxidization and tarnish with a thin coat of finishing wax.

Applying patina

1 Cover the work surface with newspaper. Wear rubber or latex gloves, a work apron, and safety glasses. Work in a well ventilated area.

2 Remove any oxidization on the solder surface by rubbing fine steel wool (000) across all seams. By rubbing across (not lengthwise), any cooling lines in the solder seam will become less visible and give the appearance of a smoother line.

3 Use a soft cloth to brush off any traces of steel wool. Discard top layer of newspaper.

4 Pour a small amount of patina into a smaller container. Apply to the solder seams with an old toothbrush, cotton swabs, or soft disposable cloth. Rub gently to achieve an even finish. Try not to get patina on the glass.

5 Clean the project thoroughly with warm, running water and a neutralizing solution. Dry with soft cloth.

6 Dispose of remaining patina (from the small container), newspaper, and cotton swabs or cloths. Rinse toothbrush in clean, soapy water.

Applying finishing compound or wax

Protect the finish of solder seams and help prevent oxidization by applying stained glass finishing compound or a quality car wax.

1 Place a small amount of liquid wax on a soft cloth and apply a thin layer over the solder seams. Avoid getting wax on heavily textured glass.

2 Allow the wax to dry to a hazy, powdery consistency. Buff with a dry, lint-free cloth until seams are shiny.

3 Use an old toothbrush or soft bristled brush to remove excess wax.

Maintaining the finished project

For normal, household cleaning, wipe the project with ammonia-free commercial window cleaner and a soft, dry cloth. If the seams have been treated with patina, they can be touched up if the patina wears or scrapes off. Solder seams left the natural silver color can be waxed and buffed again.

Replacing cracked or broken glass pieces in copper foil projects

1 Remove the broken piece using method A or B.

Method A

• Apply a hot soldering iron tip to the solder seams surrounding the broken piece. As the solder becomes molten, draw the iron tip across the solder seam, pulling the solder off the seam. Wipe excess solder off the tip and onto a water-moistened sponge. Repeat until solder seam is flat. Turn project over and do the same to the appropriate solder seams on the reverse side.

• Cut a strip of aluminum from an empty soda can and wrap one end with masking tape. (This is the end you will hold.)

• Apply the hot iron tip to one of the seams and try to wedge the aluminum strip between the broken piece and the one beside it, to separate solder between the 2 pieces. Once the aluminum strip has been pushed through the seam to the opposite side of the project, pull it along the perimeter of the piece, heating the seams with the iron tip as you go.

• When all the solder seams around the broken piece have been separated, remove piece.

Method B

• With a glass cutter, make a number of scores on the broken piece of glass in a crosshatch pattern.

• On the underside of the glass, tap along the score lines with the end of the cutter.

• Scores will "run" and break into small pieces. Remove fragments with pliers.

2 Run the hot iron tip around the edges of the entire opening, smoothing away excess solder and pulling out any foil left behind from the broken piece with pliers.

3 Place a piece of paper beneath the opening and trace the outline of the empty space with a pencil. Cut out shape inside pattern line.

4 Trace (p14) the pattern onto a new piece of glass. Cut (p15–19) and grind (p20) to fit opening. Wrap (p80) with the appropriate copper foil and burnish (p81).

5 Position the replacement piece in the opening and tack solder (p81). Continue by bead soldering (p82) on both sides of the project.

6 Apply patina (p84) to match the finish of the rest of the project, if required. Clean the project (p84) and apply a finishing compound or wax (p84).

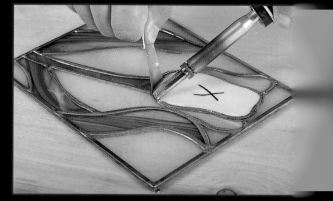

Heat solder seam and wedge aluminum strip between broken glass piece and one beside it.

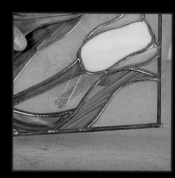

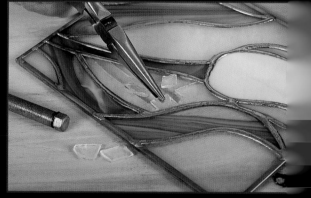

Score broken glass piece crosshatch pattern and along score lines with cutter.

Remove glass fragments with pliers.

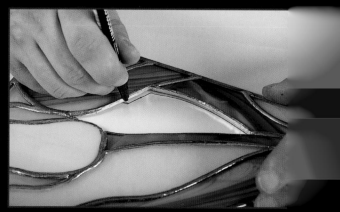

Trace outline of opening onto paper for use as a template.

Copper Foil Projects & Patterns

Salute to Spring

BEGINNER PANEL

Dimensions	7 in wide by 9 in high
No. of pieces	14
Glass required	Letters identify type of glass used on pattern (p88).

- **A**   5 in x 5 in yellow and white wispy
- **B**   1 in x 6 in green and white wispy
- **C**   6 in x 8 in green, white, and clear
- **D**   7 in x 9 in translucent white glue chip

This quantity of glass is the exact amount needed for the pattern. You may wish to purchase more glass to allow for matching textures and grain.

Additional Materials & Tools Required

Materials	Tools
silver-backed copper foil	small square
$\frac{1}{8}$ in single channel U-shaped zinc came	sidecutters
18- to 20-gauge tinned copper wire	horseshoe nails
cup hook screws	needlenose pliers
monofilament line (fishing line)	

NOTE Quantities of cames listed are based on a 6 ft length.

Instructions

1 Make 2 copies (p14) of the pattern (p88). Use one copy to cut the glass pieces. Use the second copy to fit and solder the panel together. If opalescent glass is used, make a third pattern copy and cut out the necessary pattern pieces for use as tracing templates.

2 Use the marker to trace (p14) each pattern piece on the glass.

3 Cut (pp15–19) each piece of glass inside the marker line. Use the cork-backed straightedge to assist in scoring straight lines (p18).

4 Make a jig (p80) to fit the glass pieces and keep the panel square. Verify that the 2 side trim pieces are attached at a 90° angle to one another.

5 Grind (p20) each piece of glass to fit the pattern. Leave just enough space between pieces so that the pattern line is visible between each piece ($\frac{1}{32}$ in width for copper foil projects). Rinse each piece under clean running water to remove any grinding residue and dry with a clean cloth.

6 Choose width of copper foil appropriate for thickness of glass ($\frac{7}{32}$ in is most common). Wrap each glass piece with copper foil, crimp, and burnish down edges (p80).

7 Center foiled pieces within the outlines of pattern shapes in the jig. Make sure pieces along the perimeter of the panel also align with one another along the outside pattern line.

8 Tack solder (p81) the pieces together.

9 Tin (p81) all exposed copper foil on the interior seams. Solder no closer than $\frac{1}{4}$ in to outside edge to allow space to fit the zinc came border pieces onto the perimeter of the panel.

10 Bead solder (p82) the seams of the panel.

11 Turn panel over and repeat steps 9 and 10. Because a stained glass panel can be viewed from either side, strive for even, rounded seams on both sides.

12 Using sidecutters, cut zinc came for each side of the panel, using pattern as a guide for length required. Cut each end of the 4 zinc came lengths at a 45° angle.

13 Fit came pieces onto the edges of the panel. If the glass is thicker than the came's channel, use the lathekin to widen the channel (p54, 56).

14 Place the panel in the jig. With a hammer, fasten horseshoe nails along the perimeter of the 2 edges of the panel that are not

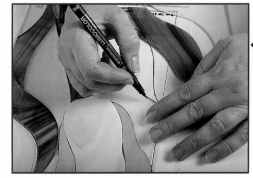

Grind glass pieces to fit pattern. Pattern line should be visible between each piece.

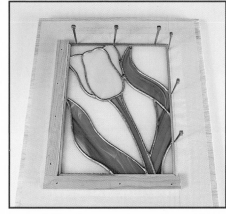

Hold border cames in position with horseshoe nails until soldered.

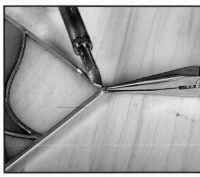

To form loops, coil wire around pencil and snip off individual loops with sidecutters.

Solder loops securely to top and side border cames.

enclosed by the jig to hold the zinc came pieces in place.

15 Solder the zinc cames in place at each point that the came meets a solder seam on the panel and at each of the 4 corners. Repeat on the opposite side of the panel.

16 To make the hanging loops for a small panel, wrap the tinned wire around a pencil several times to form a coil. Slide the coil off and cut individual loops off the coil, using the sidecutters.

17 Attach a hanging loop to each of the 2 top corners of the panel. Grip an edge of the loop with needlenose pliers and position the loop at the point where 2 pieces of zinc came meet. Apply a dab of flux to the came and the exposed edge of the loop and solder securely in place. The loop should be firmly attached to both the top and the side pieces of zinc came.

18 Cool solder joints to room temperature, clean (p84) the panel with neutralizing solution and warm, running water.

19 Apply finishing compound or wax (p84) to the solder seams and the zinc came border.

20 Use heavy monofilament line (fishing line) to hang the panel. Screw the cup hooks into the window frame and hang the panel.

NOTE Because exposure to sun UV rays can damage the monofilament, check it occasionally and replace as needed.

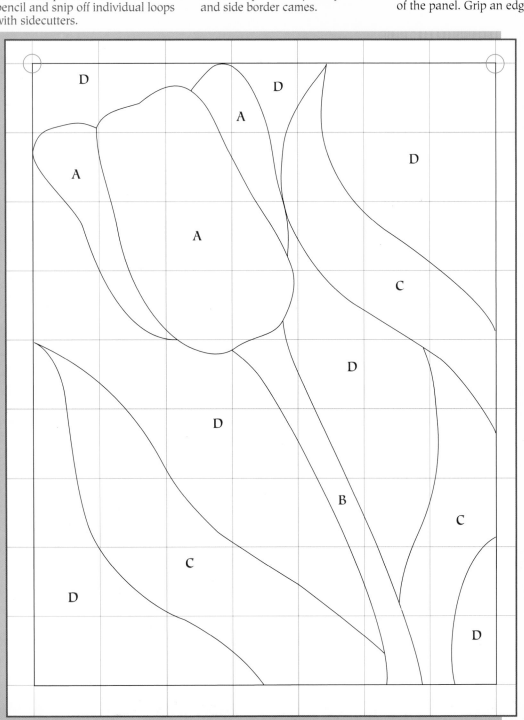

Ascending Spirit

INSPIRATIONAL PANEL

Dimensions	30½ in diameter
No. of pieces	73
Glass required	Letters identify type of glass used on pattern (p93).

A   16 in x 14 in translucent white
B   24 in x 36 in medium blue semi-antique
C   9 in x 6 in violet semi-antique
CC 6 in x 6 in dark violet semi-antique
D   8 in x 9 in white and clear swirl
E   14 in x 9 in teal green and clear swirl
F   7 in x 14 in flesh semi-antique
G   3—2 in clear circular bevels
H   Glassmith Studios' Flying Dove GST-8 bevel cluster (10 pc)

This quantity of glass is the exact amount needed for the pattern. You may wish to purchase more glass to allow for matching textures and grain.

Additional Materials & Tools Required

Materials	Tools
clear 8 mil vinyl resist	compass
black-backed copper foil	metal came bender
⁵⁄₁₆ in copper foil (optional)	(optional)
2 lengths ¼ in U-shaped zinc came	sidecutters, lead knippers,
bubble wrap and towel	or hacksaw
black patina	metal file
12- to 14-gauge tinned copper wire	horseshoe nails
heavy-duty screw hooks	needlenose pliers
linked chain	

NOTE Quantities of cames listed are based on a 6 ft length.

Instructions

Follow the same basic guidelines given for **Salute to Spring Panel** (pp87–88).

Using commercial bevel clusters

We use a 10-piece clear bevel cluster. Because commercial bevels may vary slightly in size, verify that bevels fit within the pattern lines. Grind pieces to fit or make adjustments to the pattern lines. See **Helpful hints** re: bevels (p64).

Creating sandblasted detail in the hands

Make the hands more expressive with sandblasted details and shading. Once all the glass pieces for the panel have been cut and ground to fit, cover the undersides of the pieces (F) with clear 8 mil vinyl resist (p25). Lay individual glass pieces on pattern. Use a permanent marker to trace the sandblasting detail onto the uncovered top side of the glass. Turn the pieces over and proceed to cut and remove the resist from the areas to be sandblasted (p27), using the pattern lines visible through the transparent glass as a guideline. Cover the exposed top side of the glass with heavy-duty masking tape before sandblasting the glass pieces. Once sandblasted and cleaned, the glass pieces can be foiled and soldered as usual.

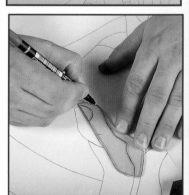

Add sandblasted detail and shading to make hands more expressive.

Layering glass pieces to create a darker shade of glass

Two pieces of glass can be doubled up to create a darker shade. To achieve dark violet glass (CC) pictured, we cut and ground 2 pieces of translucent violet glass (C) for each required piece. The pieces were cleaned and rinsed thoroughly, wiped dry with a lint-free cloth, and foiled together with ⁵⁄₁₆ in wide copper foil. Use a smooth glass such as the semi-antique suggested and burnish the copper foil tightly against the glass surface. Tack solder the pieces into position and proceed to tin and bead solder the surrounding seams. Use as little flux as possible and do not overheat the copper foil as you are soldering. Allow the solder to cool occasionally to prevent the copper foil from lifting from the glass surface, enabling flux and moisture to seep between the two foiled pieces. Before soldering the opposite side, cover the work surface with layers of bubble wrap covered by thick towels to cushion the panel. The doubled pieces of glass are thicker and will be slightly raised from the panel's front surface. Stress or breaking of the surrounding glass pieces

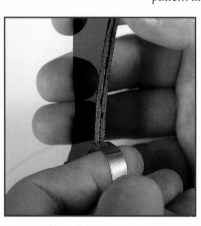

Foil together 2 pieces of the same glass to create a darker shade.

NOTE If this technique is used, double the quantity of glass required for pattern pieces (CC).

may occur if the areas around these pieces are not properly supported from underneath.

Bending zinc U-channel came to fit circular panels

Rigid zinc came gives support and strength. The circular shape of this panel requires that the came be bent. Invest in a came bender or bend it by hand, before assembling the panel. Before bending the came, use a compass to draw a sight line on the pattern that has a diameter of 30 in. Hammer horseshoe nails 3 in apart along the sight line with the flat side of each nail parallel to the line. See **Bending zinc border came manually**, p70.

Because of the panel size, you will need to form 2 lengths of came.

Assembling the panel

1 Tape a copy of the pattern to a wood board several inches larger than the perimeter of the pattern.

2 Cut (pp15–19), grind (p20) to fit, and foil (p80) each piece of glass for panel.

3 Assemble foiled glass pieces on pattern, making sure pieces align properly and fit within pattern outlines. Horseshoe nails can be fastened along the perimeter of pattern to hold pieces within the circular shape.

4 Tack, tin, and bead solder (pp81–82) the panel together. Do not solder any closer than ¼ in from the outside perimeter of the panel to allow for the zinc U-channel came that is to be fitted around panel edge.

5 Fit and solder zinc came to panel before turning it over. Because of the rigidity of the came, the ends will probably not have been curved enough to be fitted properly. Trim away one end using sidecutters, lead knippers, or a hacksaw with a fine-toothed metal cutting blade (p55). Remove any metal burrs with a small metal file.

6 Fit the came around the panel, aligning the trimmed end with a solder seam that intersects with an upper edge of the panel.

7 Mark the other end of the came where it intersects with the closest adjacent solder seam and cut the excess away.

8 To complete came border, mark and cut second length of bent came. Cut ends of the 2 cames evenly so they butt together tightly and fit snugly to the glass panel.

9 Secure the came in place with horseshoe nails around the panel perimeter.

10 Solder zinc came in place at points where ends of came meet and at each location that a solder seam intersects with edge of panel. Heat zinc well with flat side of the soldering iron tip to ensure good bond between solder and zinc.

11 Turn the panel over (see **Turning over large panels**, p59). NOTE If you have layered pieces to create the dark violet (CC) glass pieces, it is not advisable to use the edge of the table for leverage.

12 Tin and bead solder the seams on the back side of the panel. Remember to solder the zinc came to the solder seams at each point that they intersect.

Attaching the hanging loops

The size and weight of this panel require hanging loops to be secured to both the zinc border came and the solder seams.

13 Cut 2—3 in pieces of heavy-gauge tinned copper wire with sidecutters.

14 Form the loops by bending the wire pieces over a pencil.

15 Fit the loops over the zinc came border. Align the ends of the wire loops along the solder seams on the front of the panel as indicated on the pattern (p93). Allowing the top of each loop to protrude approximately ¼ in, tack solder the loops to the solder seams and to the zinc came.

16 Once the loops have been tacked into place, bead solder the wire to the seam and the came. Turn the panel over (as described above), and secure the other end of the wire loops to the zinc came and the solder seams, in the same manner.

17 Clean the panel, apply patina and finishing compound or wax (p84).

Solder hanging loop securely to solder seam and border came.

18 Screw heavy-duty screw hooks into the window frame and hang the panel using a strong linked metal chain.

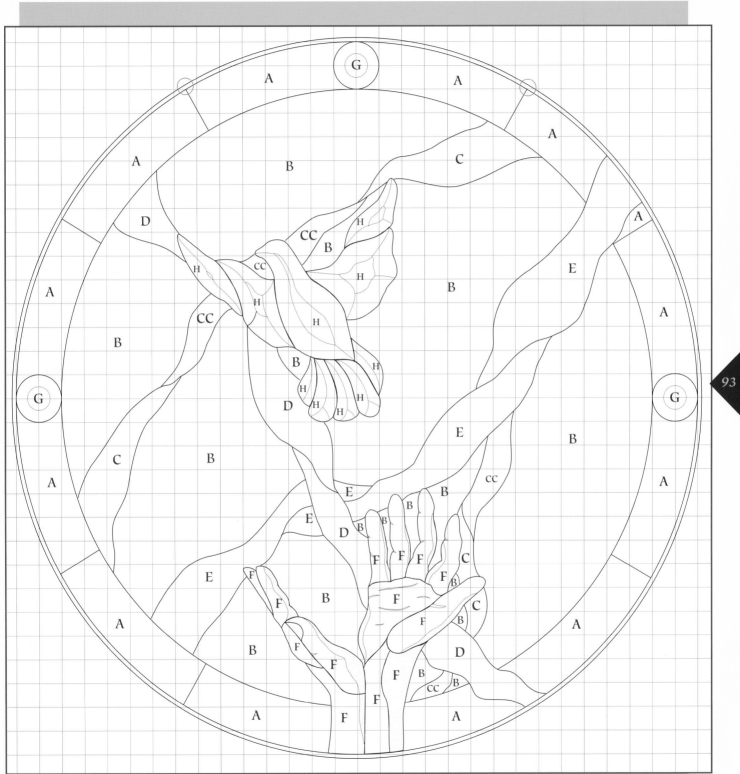

SHADED AREAS ON PATTERN ABOVE SHOW SANDBLASTED

DETAILS ON HANDS.

Harmony
LAMP SHADE

Dimensions   Height   9 in   Bottom diameter   14 in
No. of panels   6
No. of pieces   48
Glass required   Letters identify type of glass used on pattern (p97).

- **A**   11 in x 13 in translucent white
- **B**   18 in x 12½ in multi-colored streaky full-antique
- **C**   5 in x 6 in dark blue semi-antique
- **D**   3½ in x 2½ in red cathedral
- **E**   3—24mm red circular faceted jewels
- **F**   3—15mm blue circular faceted jewels
- **G**   3 iridescent clear glass nuggets (medium)
- **H**   3 iridescent white glass nuggets (medium)
- **I**   3—30mm blue circular faceted jewels

Additional Materials & Tools Required

Materials	Tools
black-backed copper foil	needlenose pliers
1—3 in circular vented vase cap	
electrical tape	
cardboard box	
black patina	
lamp base (overall height 23 in)	

This quantity of glass is the exact amount needed for the pattern. You may wish to purchase more glass to allow for matching textures and grain.

Be sure that electrical fixtures meet all government electrical standards and regulations.

The Harmony Lamp Shade, Hinged Box, and Vase are designed as a coordinating ensemble. However, by varying the color of glass chosen you can create a variety of "looks" for different settings and uses.

Instructions

This shade consists of 6 stained glass panels (alternating the 3 panels of each of the 2 panel designs) that are soldered together.

1 Make 2 copies (p14) of the pattern (p97). Use one copy as a guide to cut glass pieces to the required shape and size. Use the second copy to fit and solder the panel together. If opalescent glass is used, make a third copy and cut out the pattern pieces for use as tracing templates.

2 Use the marker to trace (p14) each pattern piece on the glass to be cut. Make sure that the grain of the glass is positioned similarly in each of the panels.

3 Cut (pp15–19) each piece of glass **inside** the marker line. Use the cork-backed straightedge to assist in scoring straight lines (p18).

4 Make a jig (p80) for each of the 2 panel patterns. Wood trim should be placed along both side edges and the top edge, leaving the bottom edge open for easy access to the jig. Each of the 6 panels must be the same size.

5 Grind (p20) and fit the pieces for one panel at a time, labeling each set with the marker.

6 Wrap, crimp, and burnish each glass piece with the appropriate copper foil (p80). We used ⁷/₃₂ in black-backed copper foil for the glass pieces and nuggets. Use a narrower ³/₁₆ in foil for the faceted jewels.

7 Solder together each of the panels. Begin by arranging the foiled pieces for one panel on the pattern in the jig and tack solder (p81) the pieces together.

8 Tin (p81) all exposed copper foil on the interior seams. Solder no closer than ¼ in to the outside edges on any seam that intersects with the side edges of the panel.

9 Bead solder (p81) the seams of the panel. The shaded areas on the pattern around the jewels and glass nuggets are filled in with solder. To prevent the glass pieces from cracking while applying the molten solder to these areas, remove the panel from the jig and place it on a damp cloth to absorb some of the heat while you are soldering. The panel must be level and the cloth should be moist but not wet.

10 Turn the panel over and repeat steps 8 and 9.

11 Tin and then solder a finishing bead along the bottom edge of the panel, leaving ¼ in from the side edges free of solder. Because the bottom edge is not even, you will have to rotate the panel slowly as you are applying small beads of solder. Allow the solder to cool and solidify for a few seconds before adding another molten bead.

12 Repeat steps 7 to 11 for each of the 6 panels.

13 Remove flux residue with a damp cloth and neutralizing solution. Wipe dry with a soft cloth. Take care not to lift exposed copper foil along side and top edges.

14 Use a solid brass vase cap with several vent holes or drill 6 to 8 holes in the cap. Clean vase cap with soap and water. Use cotton swabs to coat the top side of the vase cap liberally with safety flux and apply a thin coat of solder. To get an even coating of solder, start at the top of the vase cap and slowly draw the hot iron tip to the bottom, repeating this process until you have gone around the entire cap. The vase cap will become very hot and this will help the solder flow evenly. Handle with pliers. Cool and wash off flux residue.

15 Lay the alternating panels side by side on the worktable with the side edges touching. Align the panels so that any adjoining seams as well as the bottom edges match. Small discrepancies in the height of the panels can be covered by the vase cap.

16 Cut 18 pieces of electrical tape, 3 in long. Tape the adjoining panels together in 3 locations, pressing the tape firmly to the glass surface. Do not place tape over any of the solder seams that intersect with the side edge.

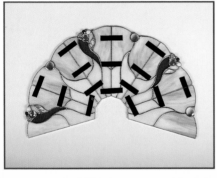

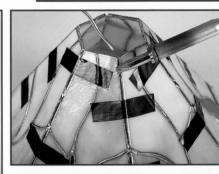

17 Pull the panels up into a cone shape by slowly lifting the top edges of the panels and matching the inside edges of the 2 end panels together, top and bottom. Using the remaining 3 pieces of electrical tape, join the 2 end panels together.

18 Tack solder each adjoining edge together in several spots and at each point where solder seams intersect with the side edges.

19 Center and level vase cap on top of the lamp shade and tack solder securely at each solder seam.

20 Remove tape and tin adjoining panel seams with a liberal coating of solder.

21 Fill a large cardboard box with crumpled newspaper. Turn the lamp shade over and prop it inside the box. Tin the 6 copper foil seams on the lamp shade interior.

22 Bead solder the seams, making sure to join the seams to the inside of the vase cap as well. It is important to prop the lamp shade at an angle that will keep the seams level while soldering.

23 Turn lamp shade over and bead solder outside seams. Touch up any solder seam

NOTE Above photos show lamp using alternate glass selection, p97.

joints (where seams on the panel intersect with the adjoining side seams), making sure they are level and rounded.

24 Turn the lamp shade upside down and complete the bead soldering on adjoining bottom edges. Check the bottom edge for an even bead along the perimeter and complete any necessary touchups.

25 Clean (p84) the lamp shade and apply patina (p84) if desired. Apply finishing compound or wax (p84) to protect and polish the solder seams.

26 Place the finished shade on the lamp base.

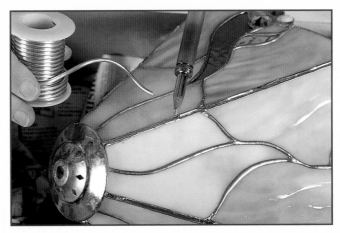

Place shade in cardboard box filled with newspaper to keep seams level while soldering.

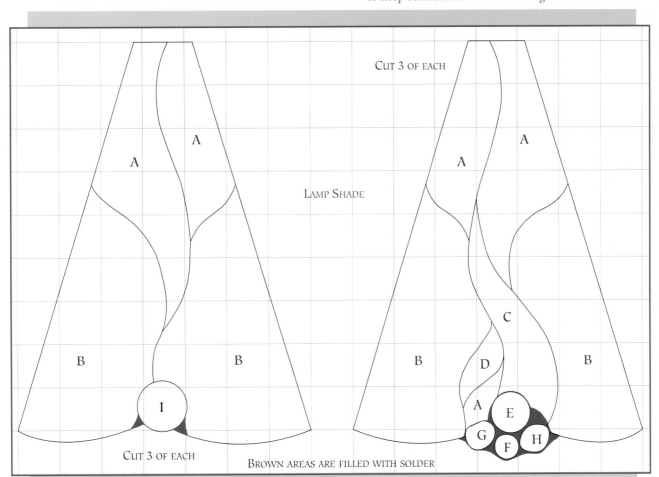

CUT 3 OF EACH

LAMP SHADE

A A A A

B B B B

I

C

D

A E

G H

F

CUT 3 OF EACH

BROWN AREAS ARE FILLED WITH SOLDER

Alternate glass selection for lamp shade

A 11 in x 13 in pale peach opal
B 18 in x 12½ in salmon and white opal
C 5 in x 6 in cranberry red cathedral
D 3½ in x 2½ in clear with orange streamers and red, yellow, and orange frit
E 3—24mm peach circular faceted jewels

F 3—15mm red circular faceted jewels
G 3 iridescent white glass nuggets (medium)
H 3 iridescent peach glass nuggets (medium)
I 3—30mm peach circular faceted jewels

Use ⁷⁄₃₂ in copper foil (regular) and copper patina.

See photograph, p100.

Harmony
VASE

Dimensions Height 9¾ in
No. of panels   3
No. of pieces   28
Glass required   Letters identify type of glass used on pattern (p100).

- A 1 in x 2 in translucent white
- B 17½ in x 9½ in multi-colored streaky full-antique
- C 2 in x 6 in dark blue semi-antique
- D 1½ in x 2½ in red cathedral
- E 3—24mm red circular faceted jewels
- F 3—15mm blue circular faceted jewels
- G 3 iridescent clear glass nuggets (medium)
- H 3 iridescent white glass nuggets (medium)
- I 3½ in x 3½ in clear texture

Additional Materials Required
black-backed copper foil
electrical tape
cardboard box
black patina

This quantity of glass is the exact amount needed for the pattern. You may wish to purchase more glass to allow for matching textures and grain.

This vase has been designed for use with dried or silk flowers only. If water is placed directly into the vase the solder seams may leak. To use fresh flowers, insert a plastic or glass container into the vase.

Instructions

1 Follow steps 1 to 13 for the **Harmony Lamp Shade** (pp94, 96, 97).
- Only one jig (p80) is required to fit the pieces of the 3 panels together since the pattern is the same for each panel. Place the wood trim along both side edges and the narrower bottom edge, leaving the top edge open for easy access to the jig. Panels must be the same size so that the vase will fit together properly.
- The finishing bead of solder is applied to the wider top edge of each panel. Remember to leave ¼ in from the side edges free of solder. Because the top edges are not even, slowly rotate the panels as you are applying the small beads of solder. Keep the molten solder as level as possible until it cools and solidifies before adding another molten bead.

2 Lay the 3 panels side by side on the work surface with the side edges ¹⁄₁₆ in apart. Align bottom edges of panels.

3 Cut 9–3 in pieces of electrical tape. Tape the adjacent panels together near the top, bottom, and middle of the panels, pressing tape firmly to glass surface.

4 Pull the panels up into a 3-sided cone shape by slowly lifting the bottom edges of the panels upwards and matching the inside edges of the 2 end panels together, top and bottom. Using the remaining 3 pieces of electrical tape, join the 2 end panels together.

5 Tack solder (p81) each adjoining edge together in several spots.

6 Fit glass base over the bottom opening to cover, not overlap, front edge of panels. Tin (p81) copper foil on base piece making sure there are no bumps of solder on the foil. Tack solder base piece to the panels of the vase.

7 Tin and bead solder (p81) all exposed copper foil seams, inside and out.

8 Fill a large cardboard box with crumpled newspaper. Place the vase inside, using newspaper to prop vase at an angle to keep side seams level while soldering all outside seams.

9 Remove vase from box. Bead solder interior seams.

10 Tin and bead solder top edges of vase where adjoining side panels meet.

11 Clean (p84) vase and apply patina (p84) if desired. Apply finishing compound or wax (p84) to protect and polish solder seams.

Helpful hint Solder melt-throughs can occur when soldering seams on 3-dimensional objects. Glass pieces can crack if molten solder drips through a seam and falls onto the glass below. Place a cloth inside the project and position it to cover the glass that lies beneath the seam being soldered.

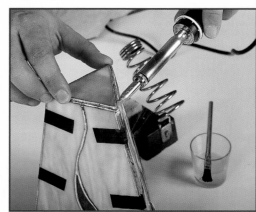

NOTE Above photo shows vase using alternate glass selection, p100.

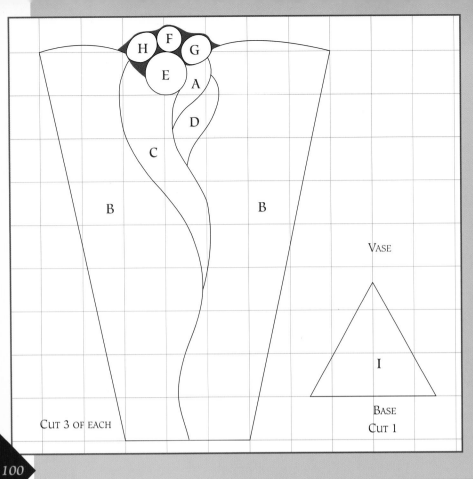

VASE

I

BASE
CUT 1

CUT 3 OF EACH

Alternate glass selection for vase

A   1 in x 2 in pale peach opal
B   17½ in x 9½ in salmon and white opal
C   2 in x 6 in cranberry red cathedral
D   1½ in x 2½ in clear with orange streamers and red, yellow, and orange frit
E   3—24mm peach circular faceted jewels
F   3 iridescent red glass nuggets (medium)
G   3 iridescent white glass nuggets (medium)
H   3—15mm clear circular faceted jewels
I   3½ in x 3½ in clear texture

Use ⁷⁄₃₂ in copper foil (regular) and copper patina.

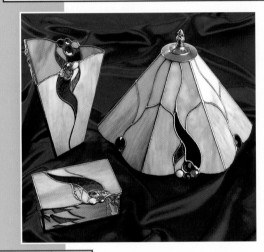

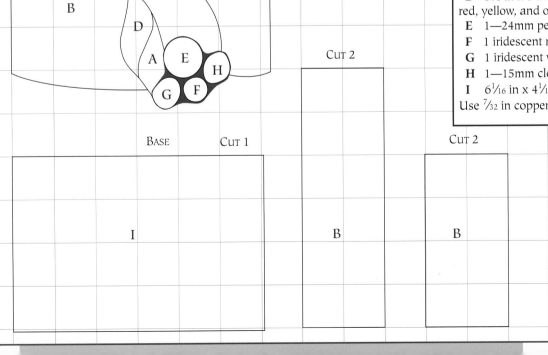

HINGED BOX

CUT 1 OF EACH

CUT 2

CUT 2

BASE   CUT 1

I

B

B

Alternate glass selection for hinged box

A   3 in x 2½ in pale peach opal
B   **Lid** 5 in x 6 in salmon and white opal
     Sides 2—2 in x 4 in clear rectangular bevels
              2—2 in x 6 in clear rectangular bevels
C   2 in x 6 in cranberry red cathedral
D   1½ in x 3 in clear with orange streamers and red, yellow, and orange frit
E   1—24mm peach circular faceted jewel
F   1 iridescent red glass nugget (medium)
G   1 iridescent white glass nugget (medium)
H   1—15mm clear circular faceted jewel
I   6¹⁄₁₆ in x 4¹⁄₁₆ in—⅛ in (3mm) mirror

Use ⁷⁄₃₂ in copper foil (regular) and copper patina.

BROWN AREAS IN PATTERNS
ARE FILLED WITH SOLDER

See **Helpful hints** regarding bevels (p64).

Harmony

HINGED BOX

Dimensions 6⁵⁄₁₆ in wide by 2¼ in high by 5 in deep

No. of pieces 15

Glass required Letters identify type of glass used on pattern (p100).

- **A** 3 in x 2½ in translucent white
- **B** 6 in x 11 in multi-colored streaky full-antique
- **C** 2 in x 6 in dark blue semi-antique
- **D** 1½ in x 3 in red cathedral
- **E** 1—24mm red circular faceted jewel
- **F** 1—15mm blue circular faceted jewel
- **G** 1 iridescent clear glass nugget (medium)
- **H** 1 iridescent white glass nugget (medium)
- **I** 6¹⁄₁₆ in x 4¹⁄₁₆ in—⅛ in (3mm) mirror

Additional Materials & Tools Required

Materials	Tools
black-backed copper foil	small file
clear nail polish	sidecutters
cardboard box	needlenose pliers
brass rod and tube hinge assembly	
wooden toothpicks	
7 in fine-linked chain	
black patina	

This quantity of glass is the exact amount needed for the pattern. You may wish to purchase more glass to allow for matching textures and grain.

Instructions

1 Follow steps 1 to 3 for **Salute to Spring Beginner Panel** (p87).

Making the lid

2 Follow steps 4 to 11 for **Salute to Spring Beginner Panel** (p87).

- Lid must be square to ensure proper fit over box. When setting up jig (p80), place wood trim along both side edges and back edge of lid, leaving front edge open for easy access.
- Use a narrower ³⁄₁₆ in foil for the faceted jewels or, if using wider foil, carefully trim back excessive overlap on edges with a utility knife.
- Fill in shaded areas on the pattern around the jewels and glass nuggets with solder. Remove lid panel from jig and place it on a damp cloth to absorb some of the heat while you are soldering. Panel must be level and the cloth should be moist but not wet.

3 Prop the lid on edge and tin and bead solder (p81) front and 2 side edges. Because the front edge is not even, you will have to rotate the lid slowly as you apply small beads of solder. Allow solder to cool and solidify for a few seconds before adding another molten bead. The back edge of the lid, where the tube for the hinge assembly will be attached, should be tinned only. **Do not bead solder.**

Making the box

4 Grind (p20) glass pieces for sides of box to fit the pattern.

5 Bevel coated side of mirrored bottom piece by holding it at a 45° angle to the grinder work surface (silver backing facing up). Beveling will help prevent chipping the silvering. Grind mirror to fit pattern. Keep the grinding surface clean to prevent scratches to the silvering. Rinse off grinding residue with clean water and dry with a soft cloth. Apply clear nail polish along the perimeter and over edges of mirror's underside to keep out flux or patina. Allow polish to dry completely before foiling.

NOTE How-to photos show box using alternate glass selection, p100.

6 Foil (p80) all glass pieces for sides and bottom of box.

7 To assemble the box, bring together 2 side pieces (one 2 in x 4 in and one 2 in x 6 in piece). The inside edges should be touching and at a right angle to each other and the mirrored bottom piece. Tack solder (p81) together.

8 Bring together and tack the remaining 2 side pieces, as above.

9 Bring the 2 halves together to form a rectangle and tack at the top and bottom edges. Each of the 4 corners of the box should form a right angle.

10 Tin (p81) the inside seams and the top edges of the box and the copper foil on the reflective side of the mirrored bottom piece.

11 Position the mirrored bottom piece onto the tacked side pieces and tack solder in place.

12 Tin all exposed copper foil except for the 2 rear corner seams where the hinge assembly rods will be attached to the box.

13 Fill a cardboard box with crumpled newspaper to hold the glass box at the appropriate angles when bead soldering (p81) all inside and outside seams. Keep the 2 rear outside corner seams free of solder. Keep the seams level as they are being soldered. See **Helpful hint** (p112) for alternative to cardboard box.

14 Bead solder top edges of box. Do not solder in the 2 rear corner edges where hinge will be fastened.

Attaching the lid to the box

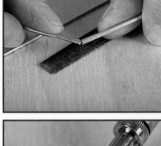

15 Remove rod from tube of hinge assembly. Measure and mark a $5^{15}/_{16}$ in length from one end of tube. Using the edge of a small file, score a notch into the tube at the marked spot. Hold the tube in both hands with the score facing away from the body and carefully snap the tube into 2 pieces. Remove any burrs from the $5^{15}/_{16}$ in length of tube with the file and set aside the other piece for use in another project.

16 Flux and tin the tube. Use wooden toothpicks in each end of tube to keep holes open. Allow to cool.

17 Center and tack the tinned tube to the back edge of the lid. Hold with masking tape, then tack in several spots. Bead solder the tube to the box, keeping the toothpicks in place.

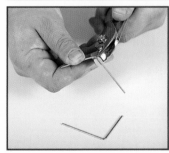

18 Using sidecutters, cut 2—2½ in lengths of rod. With pliers, grip each rod in the middle and bend in half to form a right angle.

19 Remove toothpicks and set the 2 rod pieces into the ends of the tube.

20 Place a couple of sheets of scrap paper over the back edge of the box and set the lid on top. Align the lid over the top of the box and place the protruding ends of the 2 rod pieces into the 2 unsoldered rear corners of the box. Tack the 2 rod pieces in place. Remove scrap paper and operate lid to ensure movement.

21 Bead solder the 2 rear corners. Place scrap paper at the corners (between the lid and the box) and slightly angle the box to prevent solder from running toward the ends of the tube soldered to the lid.

22 With the front of the box facing you, lay the box on its right side and open the lid. Solder one end of the 7 in chain to the solder seam closest to the bottom front corner of the box. Hold the chain in place with needlenose pliers. Place lid to maximum openness desired, and tack other end of outstretched chain to the solder seam closest to the side edge of the lid.

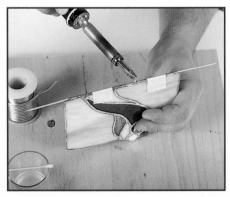

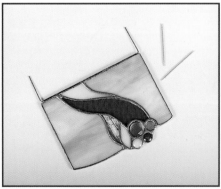

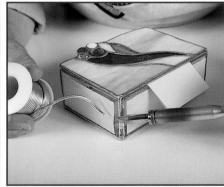

e box on its back with
the work surface.
ain securely in place.
ox and apply patina
ed. Apply finishing
wax (p84) to protect
lder seams.

Harvest

LAMP SHADE

Dimensions	Height	8¼ in		Bottom	16 in square
No. of panels	4				
No. of pieces	136				

Glass required   Letters identify type of glass used on pattern (p106).

   A   18 in x 24 in clear 4mm architectural (Cotswald texture)
   B   18 in x 16 in amber fibroid
   C   5 in x 5 in green fibroid
   D   5 in x 5 in iridescent amber fibroid

This quantity of glass is the exact amount needed for the pattern. You may wish to purchase more glass to allow for matching textures and grain.

Additional Materials & Tools Required

Materials	Tools
black-backed copper foil	needlenose pliers
1—2¾ in square vented vase cap	hacksaw or heavy-gauge
electrical tape	wire cutters
4-way brass spider	vise (optional)
cardboard box	wood doweling or pencil
20-gauge tinned copper wire	
black patina	
swag lamp assembly	

Be sure that electrical fixtures meet all government electrical standards and regulations.

Instructions

The Harvest Lamp Shade and its companion vase are contemporary stained glass designs influenced by architect Frank Lloyd Wright's classic geometric abstractions of plants.

1 Follow steps 1 to 8 for the **Harmony Lamp Shade** (p94).

• Only one jig (p80) is required since the pattern is the same for each panel. Place the wood trim along both side edges and the narrower top edge, leaving the bottom edge open for easy access to the jig. Panels must be the same size.

• Because the 4mm clear architectural glass pieces (A) are thicker, wrap these pieces with ¼ in black-backed copper foil.

• When positioning the pieces into the jig for soldering, add visual interest by turning the glass pieces (C & D) in the middle of the panel over so that the texture is facing upwards. Normally the smoothest side of the glass is topside because it is easier to cut and clean.

2 Bead solder (p81) panel seams no closer than 1/4 in to the outside edges on any seam that intersects with the side edges of the panel.

3 Turn the panel over. Tin (p81) and bead solder the opposite side.

4 Solder the 3 remaining panels, following the above instructions.

5 Follow steps 13 to 18 for the **Harmony Lamp Shade** (p96). When assembling the panels, use 16 pieces of tape (4 per side), approximately 3 in length.

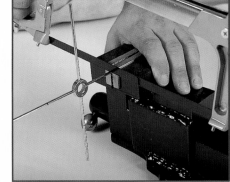

6 Before attaching the vase cap, a 4-way solid brass spider is soldered to the inside seams of the shade for reinforcement and as a way of hanging the shade from a ceiling fixture. Wash and dry spider.

7 Mark a point, 2⅜ in from the center of spider, on each arm of spider.

8 With a hacksaw or heavy-gauge wire cutter, cut each spider arm at the mark.

9 Turn lamp shade over. Insert spider, center, and line up on solder seams. Trim arms if required and coat them with a thin layer of solder.

10 Tack solder (p81) and then bead solder the spider arms firmly in position.

11 Turn lamp shade right side up and continue by following steps 19 to 23 for the **Harmony Lamp Shade** (pp96–97).

12 This shade requires additional structural support. Tin the exposed copper foil along the perimeter of the shade. Tack solder the tinned copper

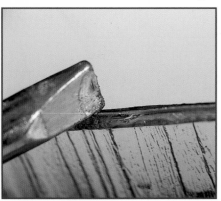

wire along the bottom edge of the entire shade, attaching it at 1 in intervals. Use a pencil to hold hot wire against copper foil while tacking around bottom. Overlap ends ½ in and snip off excess with wire cutters. Tin and bead solder bottom edge. Check for an even bead along the lamp's perimeter and touch up as required.

For support, tack and then bead solder wire around bottom edge of lamp.

13 Clean the lamp shade and apply patina (p84), if desired. Apply finishing compound or wax (p84) to protect and polish solder seams.

14 Put the swag lamp assembly and the lamp shade together, following manufacturer's instructions.

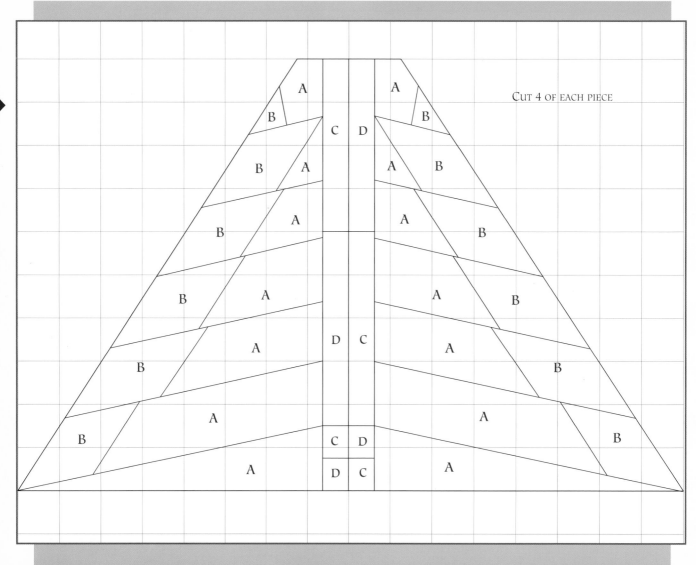

Cut 4 of each piece

Harvest
VASE

Dimensions Height 30⅛ in Width 10 in Depth 6½ in
No. of sides 3
No. of pieces 33
Glass required Letters identify type of glass used on pattern (p108).
- **A** 24 in x 37 in clear 4mm architectural (Cotswald texture)
- **B** 12 x 14 in amber fibroid
- **C** 1 in x 1 in green fibroid
- **D** 1 in x 1 in iridescent amber fibroid

This quantity of glass is the exact amount needed for the pattern. You may wish to purchase more glass to allow for matching textures and grain.

Additional Materials Required
black-backed copper foil
isopropyl alcohol
stiff cardboard
black patina

This vase is designed for use with dried or silk flowers only. If water is placed directly into the vase the solder seams may leak. If you wish to use fresh flowers insert a plastic or glass container into the vase.

Instructions

1 Follow steps 1 to 8 for the **Salute to Spring Beginner Panel** (p87).
- Make a jig (p80) for each of the 2 mirror-imaged front panels. Wood trim should be placed along the outside edge and the bottom edge of the panel patterns.
- Grind (p20) base piece and back panel to fit pattern and wrap (p80) with copper foil.
- Because the 4mm clear architectural glass pieces (A) are thicker, wrap these pieces with ¼ in black-backed copper foil.
- For variety, switch glass pieces C and D, and pieces representing kernels of grain (B), from one panel to the other. Because the panels are mirror images, the pieces can be turned over so that the texture is facing upwards and then fit into the corresponding pattern shape on the opposite panel.

2 Tin (p81) all exposed copper foil on front of panels, on seams, and around perimeter of panels.

3 Bead solder (p81) seams of each panel, with a half-round raised seam. Bead solder each seam as close to the outside edge of the panel as possible. If solder melts over edge, remove it with the hot iron tip after the solder seam has cooled.

4 Turn panels over.

5 Repeat steps 2 and 3. Tin all exposed copper foil. When bead soldering the seams, be careful not to solder closer than ⅛ in to the outside edges of the panels.

6 Turn panels over so that the front side is facing up again. Remove all traces of flux residue with a damp cloth and a small amount of neutralizing solution. Wipe dry with a soft cloth. If any residue remains, wipe it away using isopropyl alcohol.

7 Tin all copper foil on the base and back pieces, making sure there are no bumps of solder left on the foil.

8 Using front panel patterns as a guide, cut 2 pieces of stiff cardboard in the shape of the panels but 1 in smaller on all sides. Using thick masking tape, secure cardboard pieces to the front of the panels for support, as shown. Do not tape over the copper foil along any outside edge.

9 With a helper, lift and bring together the front panels. Use the base piece as a guide in matching the inside edges of the panels together and aligning any adjoining seams that intersect with the frontmost edge. Tack solder (p81) panels together in several spots along length of adjoining seam and at each point where solder seams intersect with front edge.

10 Set aside base piece. Align side edges of back piece with outside edges of front panels and tack into position. When properly positioned, the adjoining edges should form a V-channeled seam. Tack solder front panels to back piece in several spots along length of adjoining seams and at each point where solder seams intersect with outside edges.

11 With the vase still upright, run a generous bead of solder along side and front adjoining seams to add support.

12 Lay the vase on its back. Verify that the base piece fits the vase by placing it over the bottom opening. The piece should completely cover the opening but not overlap front edges of side or back panels. Tack solder base piece to the 3 sides of the vase.

13 Remove cardboard support pieces from front panels. Bead solder along the front adjoining seam (going as far down inside the vase as you can) is all that is recommended.

14 Tin and bead solder all outside adjoining seams. Touch up any solder seam joints (where seams on the front panels intersect with the adjoining side seams), making sure they are level and rounded. See **Helpful hint**, p98.

15 Verify that adjoining glass piece fits into opening at uppermost point where 2 front panels meet. The piece will angle inward slightly, towards the back panel. If required, grind the piece to fit or trace the opening and cut a new one. Wrap the piece in copper foil and tack solder into place. Tin and bead solder the seams on both inside and outside.

16 Tin and bead solder top edges of vase.

17 Clean vase and apply patina (p84) if desired. To patina the inside of the vase, pour in a small amount of patina and carefully turn and angle the vase until the seams have acquired the desired finish. Rinse thoroughly with water and neutralizing solution. Apply finishing compound or wax (p84) to all exterior solder seams and edges only.

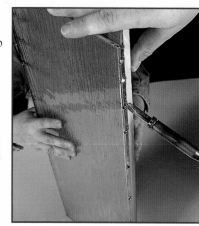

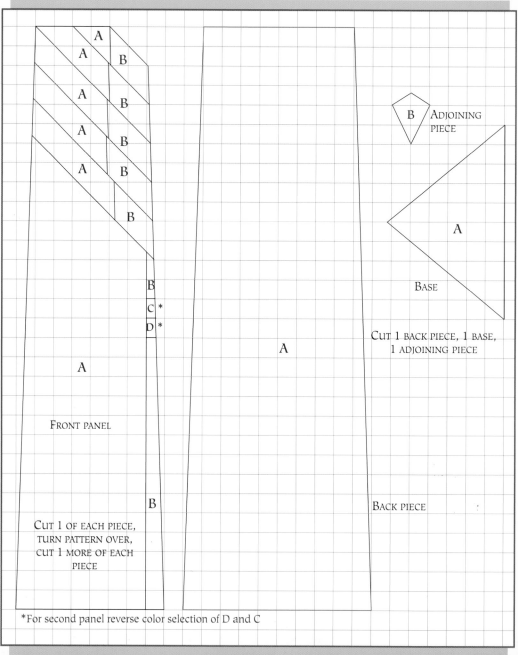

FRONT PANEL

BACK PIECE

BASE

ADJOINING PIECE

CUT 1 BACK PIECE, 1 BASE, 1 ADJOINING PIECE

CUT 1 OF EACH PIECE, TURN PATTERN OVER, CUT 1 MORE OF EACH PIECE

*For second panel reverse color selection of D and C

Celestial
CANDLEHOLDER

Dimensions   4⅛ in high by 4³⁄₁₆ in wide by 4³⁄₁₆ in deep
No. of sides   4
No. of pieces   33
Glass required   Letters identify type of glass used on pattern (p112).
  A   8 in x 3½ in iridescent cobalt blue cathedral
  B   3 in x 3 in iridescent clear with white wispy
  C   6 in x 2½ in amber cathedral textured (Niagara pattern)
  D   1 milky white moonface jewel
  E   1 iridescent amber moonface jewel
  F   2—3 in x 3 in clear glue chipped bevels
  G   4¹⁄₁₆ in x 4¹⁄₁₆ in clear glue chip

This quantity of glass is the exact amount needed for the pattern. You may wish to purchase more glass to allow for matching textures and grain.

Additional Materials & Tools Required

Materials	Tools
black-backed copper foil	sidecutters
cardboard box	needlenose pliers
14-gauge tinned copper wire	
2—18 in lengths fine-linked chain	
black patina	
snap swivel	
votive cup and candle	
metal hanger	

Safety precautions
• Never leave a burning candle unattended.
• Insert candles into votive cups before placing them inside a stained glass candleholder. This will contain melted wax and prevent stained glass pieces from cracking due to the heat given off by the candle's flame.
• In colder climates, store the candleholder indoors during winter and freezing temperatures.

Instructions

1 Cut (pp15–19) required glass pieces and assemble the small panels that make up the 4 sides of the candleholder. Follow steps 1 to 8 for the **Salute to Spring Beginner Panel** (p87). NOTE A separate jig will be required for the moon panel, the sun panel, and the 2 panels with the glue chip bevel center. Place wood trim along at least one side and bottom edge, leaving top edge open for easy access to the jig. Each panel must be the same size.

2 Assemble side panels, one at a time. Tin (p81) and bead solder (p81) copper foil seams on the front side of the panel.

3 Turn panels over and tin and bead solder seams on the other side. Solder no closer than ¼ in to outside edge of solder seams.

4 To assemble candleholder, bring 2 panels together at a right angle to each other and the bottom piece (G). There are 3 separate panel designs. To arrange panels correctly, position a bevel panel on the right and moon panel on the left, with raised surface of bevel and moonface facing outwards. The inside edges of the panels must be touching to form a V-channeled seam. Tack solder (p81) together.

5 Bring together and tack remaining 2 side panels, as above. Position bevel panel on the right with sun panel on the left.

6 Bring the 2 halves together to form a square and tack adjoining edges. Each of the 4 corners of the candleholder should form a right angle.

7 Tin copper foil along bottom edges of box as well as foil on bottom piece. Do not leave bumps of solder on foil.

8 Position bottom piece onto tacked side panels and tack solder in place. Tin all outside and inside seams.

9 Fill a cardboard box with crumpled newspaper and place candleholder at the appropriate angle to bead solder all inside and outside seams. Keep seams level as they are being soldered. See the **Helpful hint** (p112) for an alternative to the cardboard box.

10 Finish candleholder by tinning and bead soldering top edges.

To make a hanging candleholder

By adding loops and chain, this candleholder can be suspended from a metal hanger to

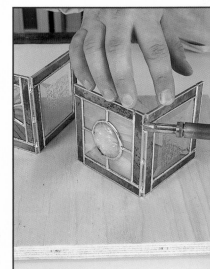

Tack solder panels together at right angles. Place a bevel panel to the right of each of the sun and moon panels.

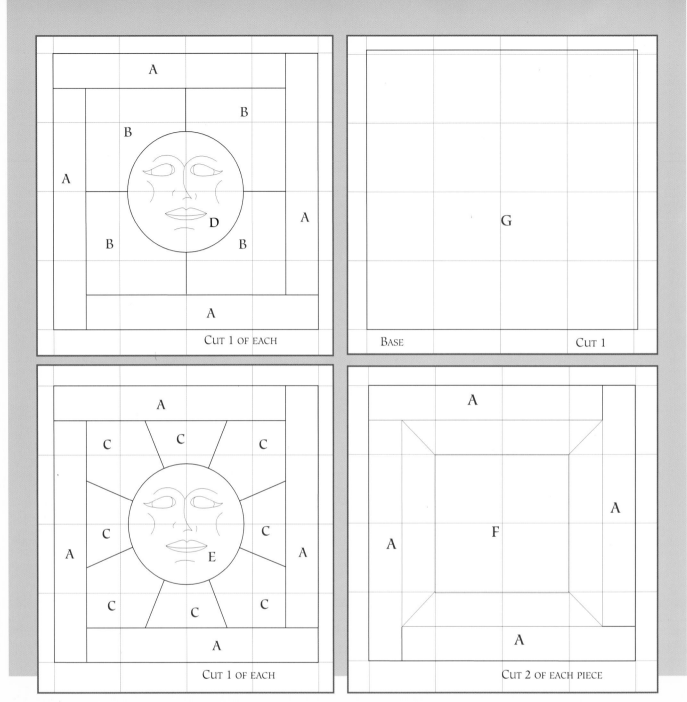

CUT 1 OF EACH

BASE

CUT 1

CUT 1 OF EACH

CUT 2 OF EACH PIECE

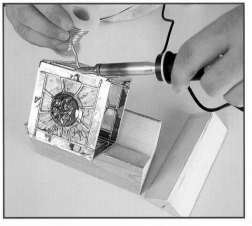

Helpful hints
• Pre-cut bevels and jewels reduce the time and effort required when cutting pieces of glass for a stained glass project. However, if the appropriate bevels or jewels are not available you can substitute a colored and/or textured glass. Place masking tape on underside and raised surface of bevels and jewels to avoid scratches.
• To make soldering smaller 3-dimensional projects easier and less cumbersome, use a wood soldering block instead of a cardboard box to keep your project seams level. On a table saw, cut an 8 in length of 4 in x 4 in lumber. Set the blade of the table saw at a 45° angle and cut a V into one side of the block. Small boxes and vases can be set into the V of the wooden block so that their seams will be level while soldering. Use the smaller V-shaped cutout when a prop is needed while soldering on other projects.

be enjoyed in your garden or indoors.

11 To make 9 hanging loops, wrap tinned copper wire around a pencil to form a coil. Slide coil off and cut individual loops off the coil, using sidecutters. See **Salute to Spring Beginner Panel**, p88.

12 To attach a hanging loop, open ends of loop just enough to slip it over one of the top corners of the candleholder. Using pliers, grip loop by the middle and hold it in place (vertically) while you tack and bead solder ends of loop to the corner seam. Attach loops at all 4 corners.

13 Attach a hanging loop on each end of the 2—18 in lengths of chain by slightly opening the ends of the loops and threading them onto the end links.

14 Slip the hanging loops from one chain length onto 2 opposing loops on the candleholder and close the ends with pliers. Attach other length of chain in the same manner. The 2 chains should crisscross over each other at the halfway point.

15 Slip 9th hanging loop onto the chains, at the junction where the 2 chains cross. Suspend candleholder by the hanging loop. If candleholder does not hang evenly, shorten the appropriate length of chain by removing some of the links until it hangs correctly.

16 For additional strength, flux and solder the links of chains closed where they attach to the hanging loops. Use pliers to keep chain taut while soldering.

17 Clean candleholder and apply patina (p84), if desired. Apply finishing compound or wax (p84) to protect and polish solder seams.

18 Clip a snap swivel onto the top hanging loop and suspend candleholder from a metal hanger.

NOTE Each design has special instructions particular to that pattern and will be described following the materials and tools listed for each one.

Additional Materials & Tools Required

Materials	Tools
½ in copper tube	pipe cutter
⅛ in copper tube	power drill with ¼ in drill bit
appropriate vented vase cap	needlenose pliers
	vice

Enjoy your garden by candlelight and be the first in your neighborhood to illuminate flowers and foliage with a stained glass torchiere. See **Safety precautions** (p110).

Instructions

To make base

1 Use a solid brass vase cap with several vent holes to allow moisture and rainwater to drain from the basin of the garden light. Tin (p81) inside and outside of vase cap by following step 14 for the **Harmony Lamp Shade** (p96).

2 Measure and mark ½ in copper pipe to the height desired for the garden light—24 in and 36 in are popular lengths.

3 Fasten pipe cutter to copper pipe at the mark. Score and cut pipe by continually turning and tightening cutter.

4 Drill a hole through the copper pipe, 5 in from one end.

5 Measure, mark, and cut a 2 in length of ⅛ in copper pipe, using the method described in step 3.

6 Clean entire surface of copper pipe for soldering by rubbing with steel wool.

7 Insert and center the 2 in length of ⅛ in copper tube into the hole that was drilled through the ½ in tube. Holding smaller piece of pipe in place with pliers, flux and solder (p81) it securely to the longer length. Heat copper pipe well with soldering iron to ensure a good bond between solder and pipe. You now have a peg that can be used to push the base of the candleholder into the ground.

8 Center the opposite end of ½ in copper pipe over opening on top of tinned vase cap and solder it in place. Ensure that it is firmly attached by soldering on both the top and underside of vase cap. Wash off flux residue using clean water and neutralizing solution.

Making the stained glass candleholder

1 Construct stained glass portion for each of the 3 torchiere designs using same basic techniques described in steps 1 to 24 for **Harmony Lamp Shade** (pp94, 96–97). Eliminate steps 14 and 15 because the vase cap is a part of the base structure and the candleholder is attached to it later. Modify the instructions to suit the specific requirements of each pattern.

2 Tin and bead solder top and bottom edges around the perimeter of entire candleholder.

Attaching the stained glass candleholder to the base

1 Hold base steady and vertical by clamping it in a vice fastened to the work surface. Check that the vase cap is level.

2 Position stained glass candleholder on vase cap. When candleholder is

level and centered, tack solder securely to the vase cap at each solder seam. Tack and bead solder (p81) joints on both inside and outside of the candleholder.

3 Clean garden light and apply patina (p84), if desired. Apply finishing compound or wax (p84) to protect and polish solder seams.

4 Buff copper pipe to a soft sheen by rubbing with steel wool or leave as is to age naturally in the elements.

Aurora Borealis

Dimensions   Height 4 in   Top opening   3⅜ in square
No. of panels   4
No. of pieces   24
Vase cap required for base   2¾ in square
Glass required   Letters identify type of glass used on pattern (p117).

  A   12 in x 4½ in multi-color streaky full-antique
  B   4 in x 4 in clear with lime streamers and green, lime, and yellow frit
  C   4—2 in clear circular bevels

Additional Materials Required
clear 8 mil vinyl resist
black-backed copper foil
electrical tape
cardboard box
black patina

> This quantity of glass is the exact amount needed for the pattern. You may wish to purchase more glass to allow for matching textures and grain.

Special instructions

Add interest to this garden light by sandblasting crescent moons onto the underside of the circular bevels (C). Once all glass pieces for each panel have been cut and ground to fit, cover undersides of the bevels with clear 8 mil vinyl resist. Lay bevels, one at a time, on the pattern and use a permanent marker to trace the sandblasting detail onto the uncovered top side of the glass. Turn the pieces over and cut and remove the resist from areas to be sandblasted, using pattern lines visible through the glass as a guide. Cover exposed top side of bevels with heavy-duty masking tape before sandblasting. Once sandblasted and cleaned, bevels can be foiled and soldered. Refer to **How-to techniques** (pp22–28) for specific instructions on sandblasting.

Shooting Star

Dimensions   Height 5¾ in   Top diameter 7 in
No. of panels   6
No. of pieces   24
Vase cap required for base   5 in circular
Glass required   Letters identify type of glass used on pattern (p117).

  A   10½ in x 10½ in blue craquel
  B   11 in x 5 in iridescent clear with white wispy
  C   6—2 in clear star bevels

Additional Materials Required
silver-backed copper foil
electrical tape
cardboard box

> This quantity of glass is the exact amount needed for the pattern. You may wish to purchase more glass to allow for matching textures and grain.

Special instructions

This garden light design has 6 panels with star bevel pieces (C) positioned between each adjoining panel. Solder each of the 6 panels together, form them into the candleholder shape, and tack solder together. Before tinning and bead soldering seams or the top and bottom edges, verify that each star bevel fits into the opening above each adjoining seam. Bevel pieces will angle in slightly, towards the center of the candleholder. Grind to fit if necessary and wrap with copper foil. Tack solder in place and finish candleholder by tinning and bead soldering all seams as well as top and bottom edges.

Polaris

Dimensions   Height 6 in   Top diameter 4¾ in

No. of pieces   18

Vase cap required for base   6 in circular

Glass required   Letters identify type of glass used on pattern (p117).

    A   6—2¾ in wide x 5¾ in high clear teardrop bevels

    B   3—39mm blue triangular faceted jewels

    C   10 in x 4½ in iridescent clear ripple

    D   3—clear 2⅞ in x 2⅞ in x 5 in triangular bevels (long half of 3 x 5 diamond)

Additional Materials & Tools Required

black-backed copper foil   wire cutters
electrical tape   needlenose pliers
cardboard box
copper re-strip
black patina
plastic bottle cap

> This quantity of glass is the exact amount needed for the pattern. You may wish to purchase more glass to allow for matching textures and grain.

Special instructions

Assemble alternating pieces of iridescent clear ripple glass (C) and teardrop bevels (A) into the candleholder shape as if they were panels. Before tinning and bead soldering adjoining seams or top and bottom edges, verify that the 3 blue triangular faceted jewels (B) fit into every second opening, at a point where 2 teardrop bevels meet. See photograph of finished piece for placement. The jewels angle in slightly, towards the center of the candleholder. Grind to fit if necessary and wrap with copper foil. Tack solder in place and finish candleholder by tinning and bead soldering all seams as well as top and bottom edges.

    This garden torchiere is designed to accommodate an optional wind guard. Here's how to make one.

1 Verify that the 3 triangular bevels (D) fit the pattern. Grind (p20) to fit if necessary and wrap (p80) with copper foil.

2 Tin and bead solder (p81) all edges of each triangular bevel.

3 Using a ½ in high plastic pop bottle cap as a prop, arrange bevels over center of cap to form a larger triangle with points on longest side of bevels touching. Tack (p81) and bead solder the 3 meeting points to form an adjoining seam ¾ in long.

4 Cut 3—2 in lengths of copper re-strip. Tin both sides of each piece and allow to cool.

5 Bend each piece of copper re-strip in half and then bend again to form a 90° L-shape.

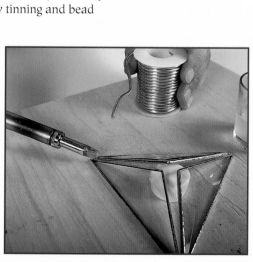

6 Turn wind guard upside down and align ends of one L-shaped piece of re-strip along the ¾ in solder seam located at one of the outer points. Use pliers to hold it in position while it is tack soldered to the seam at the outermost corner. Bead solder re-strip to seam. Attach remaining 2 pieces of re-strip in the same manner. Re-strip pieces will act as clips to hold the wind guard in place.

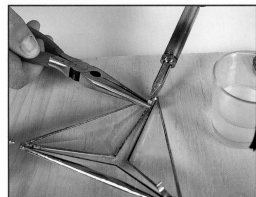

7 Clean wind guard, apply patina, and finishing compound or wax (p84).

8 Place wind guard over candleholder, as shown. The 3 copper re-strip tabs located at the corners of the guard should clip on inside the 3 blue triangular faceted jewels. If necessary, adjust tabs to fit by bending them with pliers.

SHADED AREA ON PATTERN IS SANDBLASTED

See **Helpful hints** (p112) for pre-cut bevels and wood soldering block.

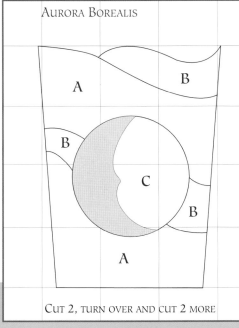

AURORA BOREALIS

A

B

B

C

B

A

CUT 2, TURN OVER AND CUT 2 MORE

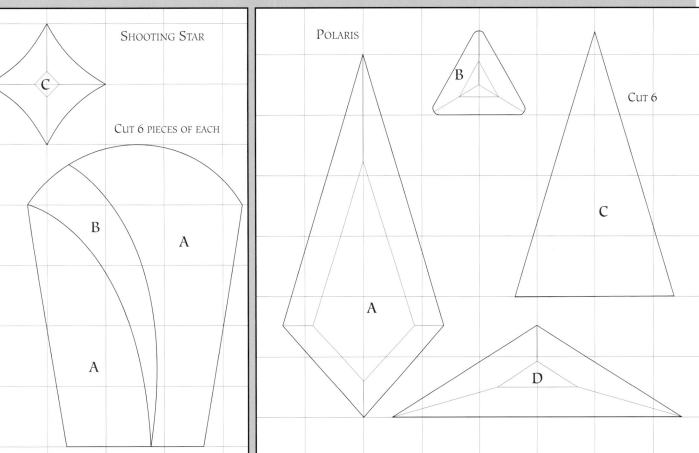

SHOOTING STAR

C

CUT 6 PIECES OF EACH

B

A

A

POLARIS

B

CUT 6

C

A

D

Patio Lanterns

NOTE Each design has special instructions particular to that pattern and will be described following the materials and tools listed for each one.

Additional Materials & Tools Required

Materials	Tools
appropriate vented vase cap	power drill with $\frac{7}{8}$ in step drill bit
commercial patio light set	small file
14-gauge tinned copper wire	sidecutters
plastic-coated cable	
plastic wire ties	

Be sure that electrical fixtures meet all government electrical standards and regulations.

In colder climates, store the patio lanterns indoors during winter and freezing temperatures.

Hot summer evenings were meant to be enjoyed. How about barbecuing on the patio with friends and family? Create an ideal setting with a set of colorful stained glass patio lanterns.

Instructions

All 6 stained glass patio lantern designs are constructed using the same basic techniques described for **Harmony Lamp shade** (pp94, 96–97). Modify instructions to suit the specific requirements listed for each pattern. Before assembly, the center hole in the vented vase caps must be enlarged to accommodate light sockets.

1 Remove the plastic shades from an inexpensive set of purchased patio lights.

2 Measure outside diameter of light sockets (common size—$\frac{7}{8}$ in). Use a power drill with $\frac{7}{8}$ in step bit to make hole just large enough for socket to fit through. To avoid compressing vase cap, drill outwards from inside of cap. Use a small file to remove any burrs around the perimeter of the hole.

3 Make lantern shades as instructed.

Hanging the patio lanterns   Once the shades have been completed, each lantern must be secured to the light set.

1 Cut 2—3 in lengths of tinned copper wire for each lantern. If required, patina (p84) wire to match color of lantern's solder seams. Bend wires at the halfway point into a narrow loop.

2 Fit a light socket through the central hole in the vase cap. Fasten lantern to the light set by fitting a wire loop over the plastic-coated electrical wire on either side of the socket. Thread ends of each loop through a vent hole on the vase cap and pull through to the inside of the lantern. Bend wire ends flat against underside of vase cap, securing lantern in place. Trim ends of wire to fit within the cap.

3 Fasten and hang lantern set on plastic-coated cable such as a clothesline or aircraft cable because of the weight of the stained glass shades. Attach light set to cable using plastic wire ties. Fasten ties on either side of each lantern and at several points along the electrical cord.

See **Helpful hints** (p112) for information of pre-cut bevels and wood soldering block.

118

Aurora Borealis

Dimensions   Height 4¾ in   Bottom diameter 3⅜ in square

No. of panels   4
No. of pieces   24
Glass required   Letters identify type of glass used on pattern (p120).

   A   12 in x 4½ in green, purple, and blue streaky granite
   B   4 in x 4 in violet glue chip
   C   4—2 in clear circular bevels

> This quantity of glass is the exact amount needed for the pattern. You may wish to purchase more glass to allow for matching textures and grain.

Additional Materials & Tools Required

clear 8 mil vinyl resist   needlenose pliers
black-backed copper foil
2¾ in square vented
   vase cap
electrical tape
cardboard box
black patina

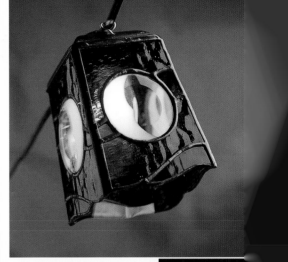

Special instructions

This patio lantern design is the inverted version of Aurora Borealis **Stardust and Moonlight Torchiere** (p115). Refer to special instructions for information on sandblasted detail on circular bevels.

Festiva

Dimensions   Height 5⅜ in   Bottom diameter 3⅜ in square

No. of panels   4
No. of pieces   12

Glass required   Letters identify type of glass used on pattern (p120).

   A   12 in x 4½ in clear 4mm architectural (Croco texture)
   B   2 green glass nuggets (medium)
   C   2 red glass nuggets (medium)
   D   2 blue glass nuggets (medium)
   E   2 clear glass nuggets (medium)

> This quantity of glass is the exact amount needed for the pattern. You may wish to purchase more glass to allow for matching textures and grain.

Additional Materials & Tools Required

copper foil (regular)
2¾ in square vented vase cap   needlenose pliers
electrical tape
cardboard box
copper patina

Special instructions

Assemble the 4 pieces of clear textured glass (A) into the basic lamp shade shape and attach vase cap. Tin and bead solder inside and outside adjoining seams. Refer to photograph and tack solder glass nuggets at the bottom openings between 2 opposing solder seams. Glass nuggets angle in slightly, towards the center of the lantern. Apply masking tape to the underside of the cluster of glass nuggets to prevent molten solder from dripping through spaces between each nugget and the clear glass panels. Fill spaces with a generous amount of solder and allow to cool. Bead solder bottom edges of panels.

Decorative soldering   Give solder around glass nuggets a decorative splatter finish. Reheat solder around nuggets, and while still molten, use a cotton swab soaked with safety flux to push solder into a splatter design. Keep adding and reheating solder and applying flux-soaked cotton swab until the desired effect is accomplished. Allow solder to cool occasionally to prevent heat cracks to nuggets or adjacent glass panels. Practice on a piece of foiled scrap glass before attempting the technique on the lantern. Always wear safety glasses when soldering, especially for this technique.

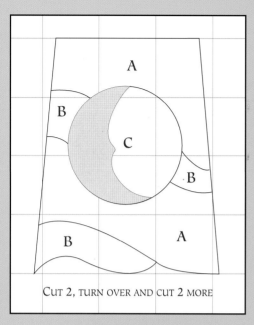

A

B

C

B

B

A

Cut 2, turn over and cut 2 more

AURORA BOREALIS

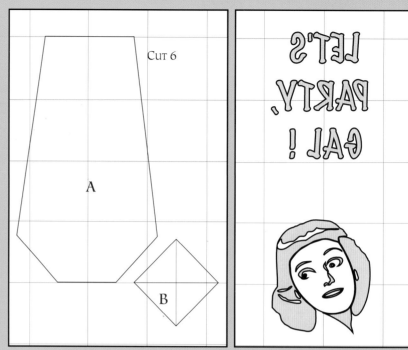

Cut 6

A

B

PARTY GAL

Cut 2, turn over and cut 2 more

A

B

C   D

E

FESTIVA

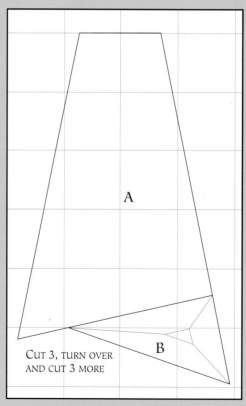

A

B

Cut 3, turn over and cut 3 more

PATIO DADDY-O

120

Party Gal

Dimensions   Height 5¼ in   Bottom diameter   4½ in

No. of panels   6

No. of pieces   12

Glass required   Letters identify type of glass used on pattern (p120).
- **A**   13 in x 4 in ruby red on soft purple flashed full-antique
- **B**   6—1 in clear square bevels

Additional Materials & Tools Required

8 mil vinyl resist   needlenose pliers

black-backed copper foil

3½ in circular vented vase cap

electrical tape

cardboard box

black patina

> This quantity of glass is the exact amount needed for the pattern. You may wish to purchase more glass to allow for matching textures and grain.

> **NOTE** Because of air bubbles, varying thickness in the glass, and the removal of some of the surface with the sandblasting process, the flashed glass pieces may be susceptible to cracks if overheated while soldering. Cool periodically. If areas become very hot, stop and allow heat to dissipate.

Special instructions

Party Gal lantern utilizes flashed full-antique glass to recreate a colorful and lighthearted 1950s barbeque theme. Cut panel pieces (A) on the thicker purple side so that the thinner layer of red flash will be on the underside. Grind panels to fit pattern. Cover red flashed side of glass with resist and then transfer the sandblasting pattern onto the resist. The lettering on the pattern (Let's Party, Gal!) is reversed because the images are sandblasted on the underside of the glass. Three panels are sandblasted with the phrase and 3 with the Party Gal's smiling face. See **How-to techniques** (pp22–28) for specific instructions on sandblasting. Once sandblasted, foil glass pieces and form them into the lantern shape with the sandblasting on the inside of the shade. Tack solder together and attach vase cap. Verify that each beveled glass piece (B) fits into the opening below each adjoining seam. Angle bevels slightly, towards the center of the lantern. Grind to fit and wrap with copper foil. Tack solder in place and finish lantern by tinning and bead soldering all seams and bottom edges.

Patio Daddy-O

Dimensions   Height 6¾ in   Bottom diameter   7¾ in

No. of panels   6

No. of pieces   12

Glass required   Letters identify type of glass used on pattern (p120).
- **A**   17 in x 5½ in blue on aqua flashed full-antique
- **B**   3—clear ¼ of a 3 in x 5 in diamond bevels (right)

   3—clear ¼ of a 3 in x 5 in diamond bevels (left)

Additional Materials & Tools Required

8 mil vinyl resist   needlenose pliers

black-backed copper foil

6-sided vented vase cap (1⅝ in side)

electrical tape

cardboard box

black patina

> This quantity of glass is the exact amount needed for the pattern. You may wish to purchase more glass to allow for matching textures and grain.

Special instructions

Assemble this companion piece to the Party Gal lantern by following the basic lamp building guidelines. For sandblasted detail on flashed glass pieces (A), see **Party Gal** lantern (p121).

Mardi Gras

Dimensions Height 4⅞ in   Bottom diameter 5¼ in
No. of panels 6
No. of pieces 60
Glass required Letters identify type of glass used on pattern (p123).

  A   12 in x 4½ in clear with blue streamers and yellow, blue, and red frit
  B   12 yellow glass nuggets (medium)
  C   12 red glass nuggets (medium)
  D   12 dark blue glass nuggets (medium)

Additional Materials & Tools Required
black-backed copper foil   needlenose pliers
3½ in circular vented vase cap
electrical tape
cardboard box
black patina

This quantity of glass is the exact amount needed for the pattern. You may wish to purchase more glass to allow for matching textures and grain.

Special instructions

The panels for this patio lantern have open spaces free of solder. When assembling a panel, align 4 perimeter glass pieces (A) on pattern in the jig and tack solder pieces together. Randomly place 6 glass nuggets (2 of each color) in center opening. Tack solder nuggets to each other and to perimeter pieces. Tin and bead solder perimeter seams and around the glass nuggets, leaving areas where there are openings free of solder. Turn panel over and tin and bead solder opposite side. Where spaces are left open, bead edges along inside opening and around nuggets to give the area a finished appearance.

Chantilly

Dimensions Height 5⅞ in   Bottom diameter 7¼ in
No. of panels 6
No. of pieces 6
Glass required Letters identify type of glass used on pattern (p123).

  A   17 in x 5½ in clear glue chip

Additional Materials & Tools Required
black-backed copper foil   needlenose pliers
6-sided vented vase cap
   (1⅝ in per side)
electrical tape
cardboard box
black patina

This quantity of glass is the exact amount needed for the pattern. You may wish to purchase more glass to allow for matching textures and grain.

Special instructions
Cut pieces, grind to fit, foil, and assemble.

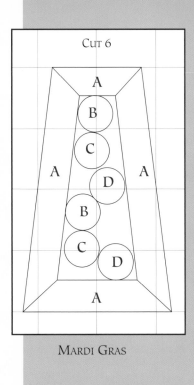

Cut 6

A

B

C

A   D   A

B

C

D

A

MARDI GRAS

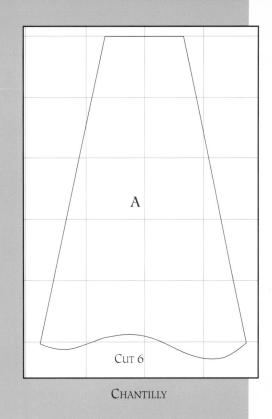

A

Cut 6

CHANTILLY

Surprise friends and family with an elegant creation using pre-cut bevels and glass nuggets.

Star Bevel Angel

Dimensions 4 in wide x 4½ in high
No. of pieces 4
Glass required Letters identify type of glass used on pattern (p126).

  A 1 iridescent light blue glass nugget (medium)
  B 2—2 in x 2 in clear star bevels
  C 1—3 in x 3 in clear star bevel

Additional Materials & Tools Required

silver-backed copper foil	sidecutters
4 ft length of tinned copper wire	wood dowel or power drill
metallic string	vise
empty solder spool	needlenose pliers

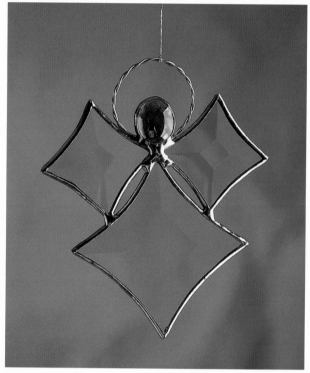

124

NOTE A power drill can be used to twist lengths of wire, quickly and uniformly. Instead of looping the wire over a wood dowel, insert the loop into the drill's chuck and tighten until the wire is firmly secured. With the ends of the wire clamped in a vise and the wire held taut, turn the power drill on to twist the wire.

See **Helpful hints** (p112) regarding bevels.

Instructions

1 Swipe edges of bevels and glass nugget against the grinding bit on the glass grinder only long enough to take off any rough spots and ensure proper adhesion of the copper foil (p20).

2 Wrap bevels and glass nugget with copper foil and burnish edges tightly to the glass surface (p80).

3 Tin and bead solder (p81) all edges of glass pieces.

4 Align glass pieces on pattern. Tack (p81) and then bead solder at each point that pieces touch one another. Turn angel over and bead solder joints on opposite side.

5 To make twisted wire for angel's halo, bend the length of tinned wire in half and loop it over the wood dowel. Clamp ends of wire in a vise. Holding wire taut, turn wood dowel until the entire length of wire has been completely twisted. Remove dowel and release wire ends from the vise. Use sidecutters to trim ends of the length of twisted wire.

6 To form the halo, wind the length of twisted wire around an empty solder spool with one end of the spool removed. Holding wire tightly against the spool, use a marker to draw a line on the wound wire from one end of the spool to the other. Slip coil of wire off spool and use sidecutters to cut coil at each mark, forming individual halos.

7 Using pliers to hold halo in position, tack and bead solder halo to back of bevel angel, as shown.

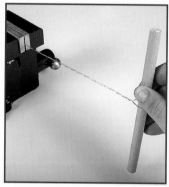

8 Clean (p84) bevel angel and apply finishing compound or wax (p84) to protect and polish solder seams.

9 To hang angel in a window or on a Christmas tree, thread a piece of metallic string through the halo and tie ends together.

Victorian Bevel Ornament

Dimensions   2 in wide x 4 in high
No. of pieces   4
Glass required   Letters identify type of glass used on pattern (p126).

- **A**   1 opalescent peach glass nugget (medium)
- **B**   2 iridescent peach glass nuggets (medium)
- **C**   1—2 in x 3 in clear diamond bevel

Additional Materials & Tools Required

regular copper foil   sidecutters
tinned copper wire   needlenose pliers
copper patina
metallic string

Instructions

1 Follow steps 1 to 4 as described for the **Star Bevel Angel** (p124).

2 Create decorative splatter soldering (p119) on front side of ornament.

3 Attach a small hanging loop (p88) on back of ornament. Use pliers to hold loop in place while soldering it securely near top edge of decorative soldering.

4 Clean ornament, apply patina, and finishing compound or wax (p84).

5 To hang ornament in a window or on a Christmas tree, thread a piece of metallic string through the hanging loop and tie ends together.

Bevel Candleholder

Dimensions   3⅞ in x 4⅞ in diamond
No. of pieces   5
No. of sides   4
Glass required   Letters identify type of glass used on pattern (p127).

- **A**   4—3 in x 3 in clear square glue chip bevels
- **B**   4 in x 5 in light blue mirrored semi-antique

Additional Materials Required

silver-backed copper foil
clear nail polish
cardboard box
votive cup and candle

> See **Safety precautions**, p110.

Instructions

1 Align the 4 side bevels on the pattern and grind (p20) to fit if necessary.

2 Cut mirrored bottom piece (B). Bevel the coated side of mirror by holding it at a 45° angle to the grinder work surface, with the silver backing facing up, then lightly grind each edge. Beveling will help prevent chipping the silvering during grinding. Grind mirror to make it fit pattern. Keep grinding surface clean to prevent scratches to the silvering. Rinse off grinding residue with clean water and dry with a soft cloth. Apply clear nail polish along the perimeter and over the edges of mirror's underside to prevent flux or patina from seeping between the glass and silvering. Allow polish to dry completely before foiling. See **Harmony Hinged Box** photograph details, pp101–103.

3 Wrap (p80) bevels and bottom piece with copper foil. Burnish (p81) edges tightly to glass surface.

4 Using bottom piece as a guide, bring 2 side bevels together to form one half of the diamond shape. The inside edges of bevels must be touching to form a V-channeled seam. Tack solder (p81) together. Bring together and tack remaining 2 bevels.

5 Bring the 2 halves together to form a diamond and tack adjoining edges.

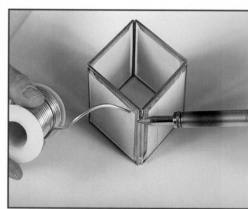

6 Tin (p81) copper foil along uppermost edges of bevels as well as the foil on bottom piece. Do not leave any bumps of solder on the foil.

7 Position bottom piece over opening of candleholder with mirrored side facing the interior and tack solder in place. Tin (p81) all outside and inside seams.

8 Finish candleholder by bead soldering all inside and outside seams as well as top edges. Use a cardboard box filled with crumpled newspaper or a soldering block (p112) to keep seams of candleholder level while soldering.

9 Clean (p84) bevel candleholder and apply finishing compound or wax (p84) to protect and polish solder seams.

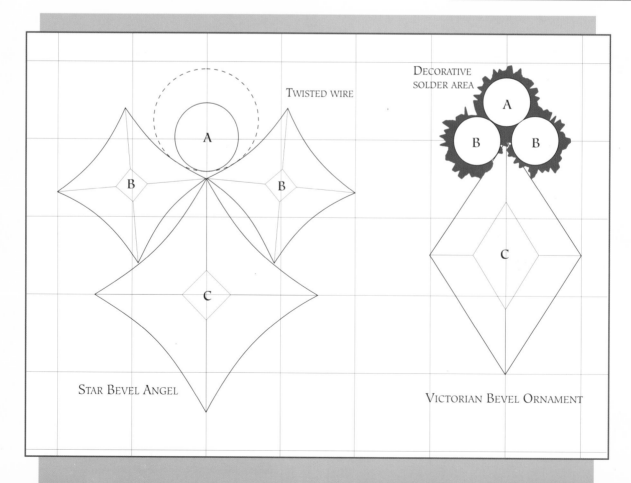

TWISTED WIRE

DECORATIVE SOLDER AREA

A

B   B

C

STAR BEVEL ANGEL

VICTORIAN BEVEL ORNAMENT

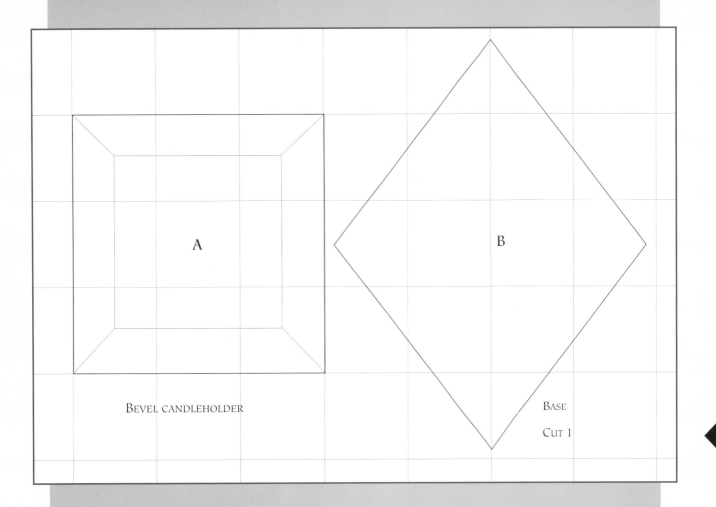

A

BEVEL CANDLEHOLDER

B

BASE

CUT 1

About the Authors

George W. Shannon and Pat Torlen began working with stained glass as a hobby but it quickly evolved into a way of life with the opening of their shop, On The Edge Glass Studio in Winnipeg, Canada. The studio offers a wide range of classes and workshops for hobbyists of all skill levels. As well as teach, Pat and George design and fabricate commissioned works for commercial and residential clientele utilizing traditional and contemporary stained glass techniques, sandblasting, and kiln work. Through the years both artists have participated in workshops given by internationally renowned glass artists. George has attended a session at Pilchuck Glass School in Stanwood, Washington. Pat recently coordinated and participated in a glass-casting course taught by Irene Frolic at the University of Manitoba. George and Pat are the authors of two other books published by Sterling/Tamos: *Stained Glass Projects & Patterns* and *Stained Glass Mosaics Projects & Patterns*.

Index